A SHORT GUIDE TO HADRIAN'S WALL

ANDREW TIBBS

AMBERLEY

For Richard & Christina. Thanks for all the support.

First published 2022

Amberley Publishing
The Hill, Stroud
Gloucestershire, GL5 4EP

www.amberley-books.com

British Library Cataloguing in Publication Data.
A catalogue record for this book is available from the British Library.

ISBN: 978 1 3981 1309 1 (print)
ISBN: 978 1 3981 1310 7 (ebook)

Typesetting by Hurix Digital, India.
Printed in the UK.

Contents

Acknowledgements

Our knowledge of Hadrian's Wall, and the surrounding Roman fortifications, is constantly growing and changing as sites are investigated, surveyed and excavated thanks to an army of archaeologists, researchers and volunteers. It is thanks to their efforts that a book like this is possible. Without the first efforts to uncover the Roman forts of Hadrian's Wall, our knowledge would be much poorer. These efforts have been, and continue to be well documented in *Archaeologia Aeliana*, published by the Society of Antiquaries of Newcastle upon Tyne and the Transactions of the Cumberland and Westmorland Antiquarian and Archaeological Society, as well as in many standalone volumes and through websites such as Heritage Gateway (heritagegateway.org.uk) which brings together historical records, as well as the Archaeological Data Service (archaeologydataservice.ac.uk), a digital archive of archaeological resources. Without these resources, this volume would be far poorer.

It has been a challenge to keep up with the latest developments in our knowledge of Hadrian's Wall because it is constantly being examined, surveyed and excavated by someone, somewhere, and therefore any errors in the interpretation or site details are mine alone.

As detailed in the book, there is a lengthy antiquarian tradition of exploring, investigating and even saving the Wall. Without those efforts, our knowledge of Hadrian's Wall would not be what it is today, and it is worth recognising the influence of those individuals on this book. Today, Hadrian's Wall continues to be one of the most studied and investigated Roman monuments in the world, and there are many researchers continuing to make new discoveries about the Wall and its function both in the Roman period and beyond. There are too many of them to mention individually, but there are some which I would like to acknowledge because their work has influenced my research; Professor David Breeze, the late Dr Brian Dobson, Professor Richard Hingley, Dr Rob Collins, Paul Bidwell, Dr Nick Hodgson, Dr Matt Symonds, Dr Andrew Birley and the team at Vindolanda, Professor Ian Haynes, Tony Wilmott, Mike Bishop, Dr David Woolliscroft, Dr Frances McIntosh, as well as the many other researchers and volunteers, too many to mention here, but who have provided an invaluable contribution to our knowledge of this northern frontier, and have helped to preserve and maintain Hadrian's Wall for future generations. A list of related publications, many of those by the aforementioned can be found at the end of this volume. I'd also like to thank Dr Paul Bennett for his patience, support, comments and editing skills.

In this book, where the term 'Hadrian's Wall' is used, it usually refers to as the Wall and its associated defences and fortifications. All the images in the book are copyright of the author, unless otherwise stated. The author has compiled the maps and contain OS data © Crown copyright and OS Terrain 5 DTM, OS Open Rivers, OS Open Zoomstack right (2021). Mapping data relating to the line of Hadrian's Wall, the ditch, and *vallum* was compiled by Nicky Garland at Newcastle University, as part of the Hadrian's Wall Community Archaeology Project, funded by the National Lottery Heritage Fund.

Introduction

In AD 122, construction began on one of the most complex and impressive pieces of engineering in the ancient world: Hadrian's Wall. It has survived wars, deliberate destruction and even pandemics. The Romans themselves tell us it was designed to keep the barbarians out of the Roman Empire, but its function was much more than a physical barrier marking the limits of the Roman Empire. It was a tool to control the local populations, a weapon to strike fear into the enemies of Rome, a symbol of the most powerful empire in the world, and it was an opportunity to collect taxes from anyone passing through the Wall, into or out of Roman territory.

What most people don't realise is that Hadrian's Wall is much more than a physical partition. It is a series of towers, milecastles and forts, spread out across a 73-mile-long barrier, with a series of defences to hamper attacking enemies on either side of the Wall. To the south and north, chains of additional forts provided support and defence far beyond

Sycamore Gap.

the military zones around the Wall. Without a doubt, Hadrian's Wall was designed to be impenetrable by enemy forces, and to control who could enter the Roman Empire.

The Wall is a complex monument, but one which has been studied and researched by monks, antiquarians, scholars, archaeologists, and everyone in-between, for most of the past 1,900 years. Our knowledge of the Wall today, and even its very survival as a physical structure, is largely thanks to those early explorers and excavators who continue to shape and influence our interpretation and understanding of Hadrian's Wall. The influence and impact of the Wall cannot be underestimated. It is not just a relic of the past, but it is also a living monument and a UNESCO World Heritage Site. It continues to shape and influence the lives and communities of those that live alongside the Wall, as well as those like myself who continue to study every aspect of this 'eighth wonder of the ancient world'.

This book is not intended as an in-depth archaeological or historical text as there are other books which more than adequately fulfil this purpose. Instead, it is a short guide for exploring Hadrian's Wall – what there is to see and where it can be seen. It is aimed at visitors to the Wall, for day trippers and casual explorers, and those interested in finding out more about the monument, and the other Roman fortifications in this part of northern England. With 2022 marking the 1,900th anniversary of the beginning of Hadrian's Wall, now is a good time get out and explore this magnificent relic of the ancient world. So, here's to the next 1,900 years.

Dr Andrew Tibbs
Durham, 2021

1. A Timeline of Hadrian's Wall

55 BC	The first invasion of Britain by the Romans takes place under the command of Julius Caesar, but the invasion has limited success.
54	Caesar leads a second, more successful invasion and establishes diplomatic ties with tribes in southern Britain. However, once 'conquered', he withdraws from Britain back to Gaul (France).
AD 40	The Emperor Caligula plans an invasion of Britain which never takes place.
43	The Emperor Claudius invades Britain. It is more successful than previous attempts, and the Emperor begins a programme to annexe of southern England, which takes the next seventeen years to complete.
60	Boudica of the Iceni tribe begins a rebellion against the Romans. She, and her followers massacre Roman citizens, burning the cities of Londinium (London), Verulamium (St Albans), and Camulodunum (Colchester) to the ground.
69	Vespasian, former commander of the invasion of Britain under Claudius, becomes Emperor, heralding in the Flavian period of rule.
Mid-70s	Roman forts at Corbridge and Carlisle are established, with others built shortly after at Vindolanda and Nether Denton. The forts at Carvoran and Brampton Old Church may also have been built around time, along with Throp and Haltwhistle Burn.
83/84	The invasion of Scotland culminates in a battle between the Romans and the native Caledonii at Mons Graupius. The Romans are the victors.
86	Roman soldiers from the Second Legion (*Legio II Adiutrix*) are sent to the Danube to quash tribal uprisings, so Roman soldiers in northern Scotland are moved to the north of England to secure more established Imperial territories. By the late 80s, the north of England becomes the furthest edge of the Empire.
100	By the year 100, the Romans have built a road, the Stanegate, across the north of England, linking the fort at Corbridge with the one at Carlisle.
117	Publius Aelius Hadrianus (Hadrian) becomes Emperor.
c. 120	Hadrian tours the Empire, arriving in Germany to inspect soldiers guarding the frontier along the River Rhine, and is unimpressed with the arrangements. He orders construction of a wall of large wooden stakes (a palisade) to be erected along the frontier to keep indigenous tribes out of the Imperial lands.
122	Hadrian arrives in Britain to inspect the northernmost frontier of the Empire. On arriving in the north of Britain, we are told that he orders construction of a Wall, 80 Roman miles long. His biographer tells us

that the sole purpose of the Wall was to separate the barbarians from the Romans.

c. 125	Construction of the forward defences, along with curtain wall, are completed.
c. 130	The rear defences, including the *vallum*, are built.
138	Fulvius Aelius Hadrianus Antoninus Augustus Pius (Antoninus Pius) becomes Emperor, succeeding Hadrian, who dies at his villa in Balae on the Bay of Naples, Italy.
139/140	Antoninus Pius orders the army to move north from Hadrian's Wall and into Scotland. The army secures the territory by establishing a series of forts.
142	The Emperor commissions a new wall to replace Hadrian's Wall. Known today as the Antonine Wall, it stretches across central Scotland, from the Firth of Forth (near Edinburgh) to the Firth of Clyde (just beyond Glasgow) and shares many similarities to its southern counterpart, except that it is constructed from turf rather than stone.
158	Refurbishment and repairs are undertaken at various sites on Hadrian's Wall.
c. 163–165	The Antonine Wall is abandoned and the Roman military reoccupy Hadrian's Wall.
c. 180	The Military Way, a Roman road, is constructed running parallel with Hadrian's Wall.
c. 181-184	Roman writers record that Hadrian's Wall is breached by barbarians.
193	Lucius Septimius Severus Augustus (Septimius Severus) becomes Emperor
208–211	Emperor Septimius Severus leads military campaigns in Scotland to crush long running attacks by indigenous tribes, but dies mid-campaign. His sons return to Rome to claim the Imperial throne, abandoning Scotland. Once again, Hadrian's Wall becomes the northernmost frontier of the Empire.
c. 383	Magnus Maximus declares himself Emperor and rules Britain, Spain and Gaul, withdrawing soldiers from northern England. His rule ends when he is executed in 388.
c. 400	A new ditch is dug at South Shields fort, and the south-west gate refurbished, possibly by local warlords or citizens indicating that life continues in and around the frontier.
410	Officially Roman rule in Britain ends, and the army withdraws, but in reality, this was a gradual process, taking place over several years.
Fifth century	Despite abandonment by Rome, the forts on the Wall continue to be occupied, with a large timber-framed hall replacing the granaries at Birdoswald, a possible church built within Housesteads, and ongoing activity at Vindolanda.
c. 540	British monk Gildas writes *De Excidio et Conquestu Britanniae*, giving a history of early Britain, including descriptions of Hadrian's Wall.
731	The Venerable Bede, a monk from Jarrow (near the fort at South Shields) writes *Historia Ecclesiastica*. Bede's accounts of Hadrian's Wall and some of the Roman forts in northern England suggests that he may have explored some of the Roman remains.
1201	King John orders digging at Corbridge to find treasures. None are found.

1599	One of the first antiquarian explorers, William Camden, visits Hadrian's Wall, writing the first substantial account of the Roman remains in almost a thousand years, while the Senhouse family begin collecting Roman objects from the ruins of Maryport fort. The collection can still be seen there today.
1660s	The Armstrong family become tenants at Housesteads farm. Notorious cattle rustlers and horse thieves, they house the stolen animals in the remains of Housesteads fort.
1725	Schoolmaster John Horsley visits the Wall. He subsequently writes one of the most comprehensive and important accounts of the remains of Hadrian's Wall. However, he dies in 1732, aged forty-six, a year before his book, *Britannia Romana*, is published.
1746	The second Jacobite uprising is underway, and an army, led by Bonnie Prince Charlie, camps near Carlisle. Despite attempts by government troops based at Newcastle to intercept the army, they cannot do this quickly because of a lack of roads. This leads to construction of the Military Road (between 1751 and 1758) between Newcastle and Carlisle.
1801	Seventy-eight-year-old poet and historian William Hutton becomes the first person since the Roman period to walk the length of Hadrian's Wall. Not only does he cover its 73-mile length from the Carlisle end to Newcastle, and then back again, but he makes the journey to and from his home in Birmingham on foot! His account, *A History of the Roman Wall*, is published in 1802.
1832	John Clayton, who becomes a pivotal figure in the post-Roman history of Hadrian's Wall, inherits the Chesters Estate and begins excavation of the fort. He excavates several sites along the Wall, and by the time of his death in 1890, he owns five of the forts and many miles of the Wall, protecting and preserving them for the future. Without his work, much more of the Wall and forts would have been lost due to ploughing and quarrying.
1840	Revd John Hodgson, who undertakes early excavations on the Wall, is the first person to claim that the Wall was built by Hadrian. Previously, it had been thought that the Wall was built by the Emperor Septimius Severus.
1852–55	The Society of Antiquaries of Newcastle upon Tyne begin excavations of the outpost fort at High Rochester, producing the first formal survey of a Roman fortification in Britain.
1870	A large collection of altars are recovered from just outside Maryport fort. Subsequent work in the twenty-first century would re-excavate the site and conclude that it was a religious centre in the Roman period.
1875	The remains of the fort at South Shields (Arbeia) are opened as the UK's first archaeological park.
1876	Coventina's Well at Carrawburgh fort is examined, leading to the discovery of many artefacts, including almost 14,000 coins.
1895	Chesters Museum, housing the Clayton Collection, is opened.
1930s	Eric Birley purchases Chesterholm (now the museum at Vindolanda) and begins excavations at the site. Around this time, Housesteads fort is given to the National Trust.
1949	The Mithraeum at Carrawburgh is excavated, confirming its original function.

1973	The Vindolanda writing tablets are first discovered.
1986	The gatehouse is reconstructed at South Shields fort.
2000	A decade long programme of excavations begin at Carlisle Castle, revealing over 80,000 Roman artefacts.
2014	The original bathhouse for South Shields fort is discovered when a pub is demolished.
2017	The bathhouse for the fort at Stanwix, located in modern Carlisle, is found during construction of a new cricket pavilion.
2021	A previously unknown section of Hadrian's Wall is uncovered by workers installing water pipes under West Mains Road in Newcastle. The discovery helps to confirm the line of the Wall to the west of Benwell fort. A new programme of excavations begins uncovering the settlement around Birdoswald fort, including revealing a bathhouse.
2022	1,900th anniversary, marking the beginning of the building of Hadrian's Wall, is celebrated.

Today, archaeologists, academics and researchers continue to explore and investigate Hadrian's Wall, and the supporting forts to the north and south of it. While excavation remains a key tool for archaeologists, it can be an expensive and time-consuming, and remains destructive because the sites are being dug. Increasingly, archaeologists are using modern technologies and techniques to analyse sites without disturbing them. Geophysical surveys, satellite and aerial imagery, and laser scanning (or LiDAR) all produce data that can be analysed off-site and can tell archaeologists much more about life on and around the Wall than ever before. Scientific techniques are also playing an increasingly important

Digging at Vindolanda.

part in not only understanding the Wall, but preserving the large of Roman artefacts recovered from the various sites along the Wall every year. Vindolanda is the best place to see digging in action, as the ground conditions at the site preserves organic items such as wood, leather, cloth, writing tablets and occasionally hair (there's an original Roman wig made from hair on display in the museum). Once excavated, organic items can fall apart quickly if they are not put through a process of preservation, a scientific method that Vindolanda are very adept at. Some of the organic items recovered from the site can be seen in the museum, including hundreds of Roman shoes. Many of the museums along the Wall undertake research into both their own sites and the objects found at them, and undertake regular exhibitions.

Traditional excavation still has a major role to play in enhancing our understanding of Hadrian's Wall and the forts. One of the largest and longest running excavations takes place at Vindolanda fort, with volunteers travelling from around the world to take part. The excavation season starts in early April and goes on until the end of September. Unlike most of the other research programmes and excavations which take place on the Wall, anyone can sign up to excavate at Vindolanda, although places are competitive and go within a short time of being advertised (usually in the autumn of the preceding year). Visiting the on-site museum, as mentioned above, gives an insight into some of the amazing finds that have been recovered from the site, almost all of them found by volunteer excavators. Although there are no organised excavations at the Roman fort of Carvoran, the site owners, the Vindolanda Trust, are planning a series of investigations at the fort aimed at checking the preservation levels as the water levels seem to have dropped in recent years threatening some of the archaeology. The Vindolanda website will give details on any excavations that the public can visit at Carvoran.

At the western end of the Wall, English Heritage are working with Newcastle University to excavate around the fort at Birdoswald. The work, undertaken by students, focuses on the civilian settlement around the fort, and takes place in the early summer months over several years. Guided tours of the excavations take place daily when the teams are on site, with more details on the English Heritage website. Recent excavations have also taken place at Carlisle, in the grounds of the Cricket Club where the bathhouse for Stanwix fort has been uncovered. The excavations will take place over several years during the summer months, with visitors able to tour the site.

Additional excavations occasionally take place on other sites along the Wall, usually in the urban areas where sites are found during other works. These excavations are brief and there is limited access for visitors, but it is worth checking local media for more details when there are discoveries made.

2. A Short Overview of Hadrian's Wall

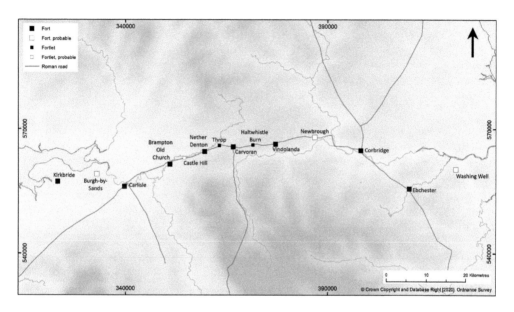

The Stanegate fortifications. (N. Garland, 2020 – CC BY-NC-SA 4.0)

The Stanegate

The story of Hadrian's Wall really begins before AD 122, before the arrival of Hadrian in Britain, and before the orders were given to construct a barrier to separate the Barbarians from the Romans. Sometime around AD 100, but possibly as much as twenty years before, the Roman General Julius Gnaeus Agricola had taken over the governorship of Britain and had been campaigning voraciously, conquering Wales before moving his forces northwards with his eye on Scotland. Around the early AD 70s, the Roman military, a little before Agricola's tenure, arrived at what became Carlisle, beginning construction of the fort that now lies partly underneath Carlisle Castle. This dating has been confirmed from dendrochronology or tree dating of timbers used in the construction of the fort. Only a few years later, they would do the same at Corbridge, building the first fort that would control the crossing over the River Tyne. The dating of that site is a little less clear, but archaeologists know with some certainty that it had been established by the mid-70s. One issue the military faced was the difficulty in quickly and efficiently crossing the crags and moors between the two forts. This also seems to have been a strategic issue in the post-Roman period until the construction of the Military Road, an eighteenth-century road running between Newcastle and Carlisle and follows the line of Hadrian's Wall (sometimes literally on top of it) for a large part of its route. For the Romans, the solution was to construct a road running between Corbridge and Carlisle, which was most likely built under the orders of Agricola to aid his campaigns in northern Britain, or possibly by one of his successors, and more or less marked the northernmost edge of the Empire, although for how long is not known. After the construction of the first two forts in the east and west, additional ones were built in-between, at Vindolanda and Nether Denton by the mid-80s. At the beginning of the second century, unrest elsewhere in the Empire seems to have led to a reorganisation of the military in Britain, and this is probably when additional forts, at Carvoran and Brampton Old Church were constructed, with a number of smaller fortifications, known as fortlets built at Newbrough, Haltwhistle Burn, Throp, and Boothby, along with several towers towards the western end of the fort at Barcombe Hill, Birdoswald, Mains Rigg and Pike Hill. Archaeologists think this shows a strengthening of the Stanegate as a frontier, or an attempt to secure the limits of the Empire. The fortifications on the line are fairly regularly spaced out, and this could indicate a desire by the army to have troops more evenly spaced along the Stanegate, enabling more flexibility and quicker response times when dealing with threats.

Archaeologists often speculate that the Stanegate road went further east and west, beyond Carlisle and Corbridge, but so far no evidence has been found of this. There are Roman forts beyond these Carlisle and Corbridge. The fort at Kirkbride, to the south-west of Carlisle, dates to the same period as the other Stanegate forts, and the line of a possible Roman road has been traced leaving the eastern gate of the site. On the other side of the country is the fort at Washing Wells (by Whickham), which is to the south-east of Newcastle, but remains undated and no roads have yet been identified. None of this proves or disproves the original extent of the Stanegate, but it shows that there is much more to discover about the early Roman sites in Northern England.

Hadrian's Wall

Stretching between the River Tyne and the Solway Firth, Hadrian's Wall is much more than a wall of stones. It is a series of defensive structures and fortifications that together make up what can best be described as a complex. To be more specific, there is a ditch, the berm (a small mound at the edge of the ditch), pits with thorns or spikey poles sticking out of them, three types of Wall depending on the location (the physical wall is often referred to as the curtain wall to distinguish it from the wider Hadrian's Wall complex), a possible road, a super wide ditch known as the *vallum*, and a road.

Interspersed at regular intervals are a series of forts, which are the main bases for the soldiers patrolling the Wall. Between these are smaller fortifications built into the physical wall known as milecastles, and between those are two towers or turrets. The Romans were master engineers, making use of the natural terrain to support their structures, and Hadrian's Wall is no except as it follows the river valleys of the Tyne and Irthing, but within that landscape takes advantage of the many craggy outcrops which run through the region.

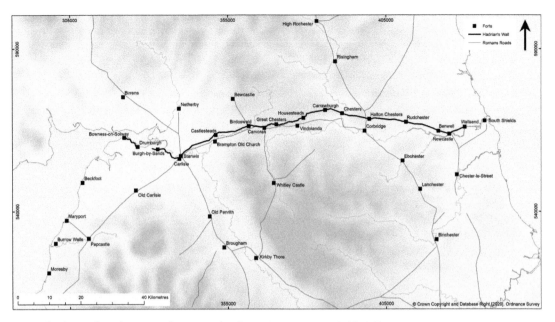

The forts of Hadrian's Wall. (N. Garland, 2020 – CC BY-NC-SA 4.0)

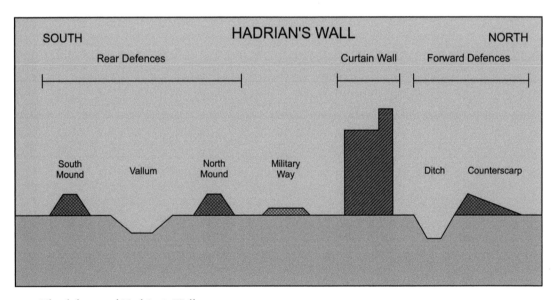

The defences of Hadrian's Wall.

Often this means that the *vallum*, the larger and wider ditch which runs to the south of the Wall, can be quite a distance from the Wall itself particularly in the central section.

The construction of such a substantial monument was a complex process, with the overall design changing on several occasions. The initial plan had no forts constructed on the line of the Wall, and instead would have made use of the Stanegate forts, housing the soldiers there. There was to have been milecastles every Roman mile, with a secure opening through the Wall itself, which in the western sector was going to be constructed from turf, along with the fortification. However, before the Wall was completed, the plan was drastically changed, with the width of the Wall reduced and forts were introduced at around 11-kilometre gaps, with forts placed astride or over the line of the Wall. This occurred during construction as parts of the Wall have been excavated underneath forts, while the remains of milecastles and turrets have also been found beneath them, showing that they were demolished for the forts to be built.

Forward Defences

In front of the curtain wall are a group of forward defences, a line of nasty surprises, each designed to slow down attacking enemies, potentially inflicting painful and even fatal injuries. How often the Wall was attacked is not known, but there is some suggestion from Roman writers that it was breached in its later history, but it isn't clear where or when, and no archaeological evidence of a breach or battle has been uncovered. The Wall itself would have been an intimidating site to an indigenous population who had never seen any sort of monumental engineering, and certainly nothing on the scale and complexity of the Wall. There is also some evidence, although it is not conclusive, that the Wall may have been covered in a whitewash, which would only have added to the intimidating appearance of the structure in the eyes of the locals already living in the north of England before the Romans.

Wall and ditch by Limestone Corner.

Furthest from the Wall is the counterscarp, sometimes known as the glacis, and is a mound built up on top of the northernmost edge of the ditch to make the defences look more impressive to anyone approaching it. Behind this was the ditch, a V-shaped defensive feature found surrounding most Roman fortifications, although most of those have a standard width and depth all around an individual fort, but on the Wall this varies. The average depth was just under 3 metres while the width was an average of just over 8 metres wide, making it a substantial obstacle to be overcome, especially as the sides were quite steep and would have been difficult for attackers to climb out of. The soil gathered from digging the ditch was piled up on the north side to create the counterscarp.

Between the ditch and the Wall is the berm, which is a wide, empty area about 6 metres wide. Evidence from the eastern section of the Wall has recorded a series of shallow ditches, which have been described as emplacements for thorns and branches, above ground obstacles designed to slow down attackers. While there is evidence for this occurring along the eastern end of the Wall, there is no evidence for them anywhere else, although it may be because archaeologists haven't yet looked for them.

The Walls

Often referred to as the curtain wall to distinguish it from the wider Hadrian's Wall complex, it is not well known that there are actually three different walls, which were built in different locations – a Turf Wall, a Broad Wall, and a Narrow Wall. The initial building of Hadrian's Wall saw a wall built from turf in the west, with a broad, wide wall in the east, with the former replaced in stone, and the latter reduced in width during construction.

The Turf Wall, which ran from the River Irthing by Birdoswald to the western terminus at the fort at Bowness-on-Solway, was constructed straight onto the ground, with turf slabs or turves laid directly on top of each other. At the bottom, the width of the wall was around 6 metres wide, with the front face having a steep incline, while the rear one was much gentler. There is speculation that there was a wooden walkway along the top of the Wall enabling soldiers to patrol it, and although there is no evidence to support this, it seems like a sensible addition to the Wall. Besides the Wall, the early fortifications had turf walls, with timber buildings built on turf foundations. Eventually the Wall and the fortifications were all replaced in stone, although in some places the replacement stone wall was on a slightly different alignment to its turf predecessor, with this being most visible between Milecastles 49 (Harrow's Scar) and 51 (Wall Bowers), both near Birdoswald fort, and where the Wall is slightly north of the line of the Turf Wall, with the latter surviving to the north of the *vallum*.

The Broad Wall, running between Newcastle and the River Irthing by Birdoswald, was built similarly, with large foundation stones placed on a bed of clay, while the outer stones on the lower levels were bonded together with clay, and occasionally mortar. The outer stones were dressed or finished to be square or rectangular shaped, fitting together perfectly while the inner core of the Wall comprised whatever was nearby, boulders and river stones. The Broad Wall was just over 3 metres in width, but after the first couple of courses were laid, the plan changed and width was reduced to create the Narrow Wall, which varies in width between 1.8 and 2.3 metres in width. In some places, due to the change in design of the Wall, the Narrow Wall uses the incomplete Broad Wall as its own foundations, as seen at Willowford.

Narrow Wall
on Broad Wall
foundations, Willowford.

There is also an additional section of Wall at the western end by Bowness fort and Milecastle 54, which is of a fourth different design. Known as the Intermediate Wall, it was built on a stone base and is around 2.4 metres wide, although this is the only section of Hadrian's Wall that this width occurs.

Rear Defences

To the rear of the curtain wall, on the south side, are a series of additional defences, designed to both slow down any attackers breaching the Wall, but also help to speed up the Roman response and general movement through the area. Closest to the Wall itself are

South mound (left), *vallum* (centre), and north mound (right), near Limestone Corner.

the remains of the Military Way, a Roman road that archaeologists think was built after the main period of Wall building because in places the road appears to run on top of the north mound of the *vallum*. Some archaeologists have speculated that the road dates to the time that Hadrian's Wall was reoccupied after it had been abandoned in favour of the Antonine Wall.

It is worthwhile noting the distinction between the Military Way (the Roman road behind the curtain wall) and the Military Road, the eighteenth-century route, which links Newcastle and Carlisle, and was built to make the journey between the two locations easier and quicker. Previously, the journey had taken the army the best part of a week. Around 30 miles of the eastern section of the Wall was demolished, and its foundations were used for the base of the Military Road. This was despite the protestations of antiquarians who argued the government routes should follow the line of the old Roman roads. Today, you can still follow the general line of the Military Road between Newcastle and Carlisle, and for part of the route drive on top of the remains of Hadrian's Wall by following the modern A186, then onto the A69 briefly before taking the B6318 for a large part of the route, then onto the A69, the A689 and onto B6264 and into Carlisle.

To the south of the Military Way is the most substantial part of these defences, the *vallum*, a curious feature which is a particularly wide, but not deep, although it varies depending on the natural topography. The *vallum* is around 6 metres wide in most places where it has been located, and 3 metres deep. It seems to have run for most of the length of the Wall, starting at Newcastle in the east (not at the easternmost fort on the Wall at Wallsend) and finished at Bowness, although in some places the line of the *vallum* remains unknown. Some forts were built on top of the *vallum*, while at others, it runs around the southern end of the fortifications. There were regular crossing points over the *vallum*, such as the one that can still be seen at Benwell (Newcastle), where a large gate sat on top of the crossing which enabled the army to control, who could access the space between the *vallum* and the fort and Wall.

To the north and south of the *vallum* are a pair of mounds made from the contents of the *vallum* when it was dug. In some places, there's an additional mound on the southern edge of the *vallum*. Known as the marginal mound, it seems to have only been created in a few places and doesn't always occur. At Milecastle 50 (known as Turf Wall), archaeologists have found evidence of a track on top of the south mound. It's not clear if this was a feature, which was only built along this section of the Wall, or something which extended further. There is also some evidence of a road surface on top of the north mound in some places, but again this is limited and it's not clear if this is a localised feature or something more substantial.

Fortifications

The largest type of fortifications that the Romans built in northern England were forts. These were local bases that housed the soldiers and had a range of administrative, religious and financial functions. The Roman army was divided into legionary soldiers (Roman citizens in the army) and auxiliary soldiers (non-Roman citizens), with the former responsible for construction of the Wall, and the latter patrolling and guarding it. The forts are usually similar in size, accommodating around 500 infantry and cavalry (mounted soldiers), although at the smaller end (Carvoran and Great Chesters) would only have housed 500 infantry, while the largest at Stanwix would have housed 1,000 cavalry.

Forts were built to a similar plan, although there were variations depending on the units based at each site, and over time additional buildings were constructed and the basic site plan varies. A good example of this can be seen at South Shields, which started out as a standard fort housing cavalry, but by the second and third centuries most of the barracks had been knocked down and replaced with granaries and it became a supply base to support campaigning in Scotland. There are seventeen forts that can be considered part of the Hadrian's Wall complex, although two of these, Vindolanda and Carvoran, are on the Stanegate and were in use not only before construction of the Wall, and continued in operation during the Hadrianic period.

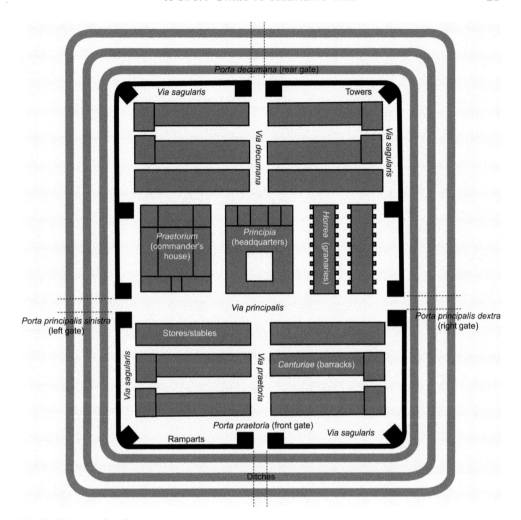

Typical Roman fort layout.

The original construction plan for the Wall omitted forts and instead had the smaller fortifications, the milecastles, every Roman mile, with turrets in between. The milecastles were small, self-contained fortifications that were bases for soldiers patrolling the relevant sections of the Wall. They also acted as secured routes through the Wall, with gates, controlled by the soldiers, opening into the space north of the Wall. From excavated evidence, archaeologists have concluded that there were no plans for forts on the Wall initially because the remains of milecastles and turrets are underneath the forts at Housesteads, Great Chesters and Bowness. There are also some turrets which were built before the Wall. These turrets were designed to connect to the Broad Wall, but between these being built and the Wall being connected to them, the design changed from the Broad Wall to the Narrow Wall. At these sites, the turret sections of connecting wall are noticeably wider than the Wall itself. Due to the changes in construction, and despite attempts by archaeologists to locate them, the actual number of the milecastles and turrets remains unknown.

The Coastal Defences

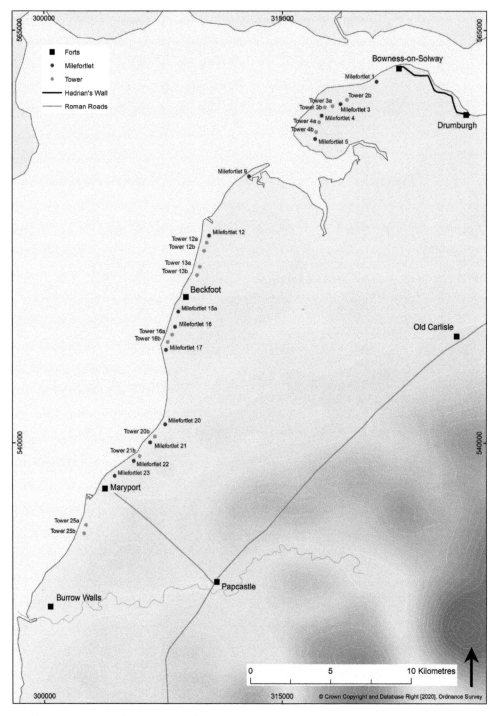

Cumbrian Coastal Defences. (N. Garland, 2020 – CC BY-NC-SA 4.0)

Hadrian's Wall was the central feature of a series of regional defences built by the Romans and which stretch across northern England and beyond. To the west, beyond the end of the Wall at Bowness-on-Solway, a series of defences were constructed along the Cumbrian coast stretching to the south of Maryport fort. Sharing some similarities, the Cumbrian coastal defences comprise a series of forts interspersed with mile fortlets (similar to the milecastles), and turrets in between these. But, unlike Hadrian's Wall, there is no firm evidence of a barrier running between these fortifications, and there's no evidence of the mile fortlet and turret arrangement extending to the most southern fort on the Cumbrian coast at Ravenglass

The Outpost Forts

To the north of Hadrian's Wall, there are a few forts that were occupied at the same time as the Wall, which acted as outposts. Soldiers at these forts would have been able to intercept trouble and quell unrest from the indigenous tribes and provide an initial layer of defence for the Wall. These forts would also have been bases for scouting trips and explorations of the territory to the north, and would have also provided valuable intelligence for the commanders behind the Wall.

3. Life and Death on Hadrian's Wall

The main purpose of the Wall was clear – to keep the barbarians out of the Empire – but Hadrian's Wall was much more than this. For those who followed the army, the traders, the crafters and those who supplied the military with extra goods and services, the Wall would have been a lucrative opportunity. Communities developed around the Wall, and many goods and services could be found within these – pubs, temples and everything in between. For the wives, children, slaves and other family members who followed the army around the Empire, the Wall would have been an opportunity to be close to their loved ones. There is even evidence of tourism associated with the Wall. For those living in the north before the Romans arrived, the Wall was a barrier that cut through their lands and divided families. Some may have risen up against the Roman army and their monumental

Regina tombstone replica, South Shields.

symbol of oppression, and probably not survived for long, but for others they may have taken advantage of the new opportunities and sought the protection of Rome, and may even have been some of the earliest residents of the new settlements by the forts.

Indigenous Settlements

It is Hadrian's biographer who states the reason for building the Wall, and apart from this account, there are very few surviving Roman records that talk about the impact of the Wall on the indigenous population, although one tablet recovered from Vindolanda describes the locals as 'wretched little Brits'. Instead, we have to rely on the archaeology to tell us what the landscape was like before the building of the Wall and its impact on the local population.

What is known, from Roman writers (who may have been biased in their views), is that the indigenous population grouped together into tribes, which are best described as social groupings. Some tribes controlled small area, but other tribal lands extended for hundreds of miles, and construction of the Wall cut across some of these territories. The establishment of the Wall also seems to have created a military zone around the structure, which was probably a 'no go' area for non-military personnel. Archaeologists know this because of one indigenous site to the west of Housesteads fort at Milking Gap. Archaeologists have excavated the land beneath several Wall sites and have concluded that, before its construction, most of the land was ploughed by the indigenous population. The site at Milking Gap, an indigenous farm, seems to have been abandoned when construction begins, probably because it found itself between curtain wall and the *vallum*, although it's not clear if the occupants were forced out by the Romans, or decided that it was best to vacate the site on their own accord. It seems unlikely that there was a wholesale clearance of the territories around the Wall, only the adjacent lands, as the Romans would have needed food for the soldiers and horses and it would have been easier to allow the locals to continue farming, and for the army to take a cut of the produce. This would have also enabled the military to focus on construction and patrolling the war instead of having soldiers undertake farming duties.

With construction of the Wall, there appears to have been an increase in development to the south of the structure, such as villas in County Durham – rather than being the grand, luxury buildings that are seen in southern England and elsewhere in the Empire, the ones in the north were more like farmhouses. There also seems to have been an increase in roundhouses, traditional indigenous homes, which may indicate migration of the local tribal populations to be closer to the Wall itself, partly for protection but possibly because of the economic benefits of being near the army.

Roman Settlements

Soon after, or possibly even during construction of Hadrian's Wall, settlements were established around the forts, both on the Wall and on the Cumbrian coast, although there is

Civilian settlement remains, Housesteads.

a lack of evidence for these around the more remote and probably more dangerous outpost sites. Settlements were mixed communities and provided a home for families of the soldiers, retired soldiers, and many craftspeople, traders and those providing services. The writing tablets discovered at Vindolanda, and produced around AD 92–103, highlight some of the supplies requested by those in the fort from traders. Goods include things such as beer and hides (brought from Catterick). Archaeologists have also uncovered artefacts that suggest that blacksmiths and potters were producing goods in the settlements, with traders importing objects from further afield.

The settlements can best be compared to shantytowns, mainly composed of timber buildings, often built on turf foundations making them damp and particularly prone to the challenging weather experienced on the Wall. At some sites, such as Housesteads and Vindolanda, some of the building had the luxury of stone foundations. These settlements lacked necessities such as plumbing, with most buildings interconnected by mud tracks rather than the formal roads the Romans are known for. This also shows the differences between the settlements surrounding the forts and more developed towns such as Corbridge where the roads were properly surfaced and there were drains to take away excess water and sewage. Water was even piped into the heart of the town and freely available from an ornate fountain on the main street.

Settlements varied in size, although few have been extensively excavated. Carlisle fort seems to have the most extensive settlement, although knowledge of it is limited by the modern city, and there are only glimpses of it when development takes place and uncovers pockets of remains. Housesteads is another site with a large settlement, with more than twenty-seven buildings uncovered during excavations in the 1930s, with more remaining hidden beneath the soil. The fort at Birdoswald also appears to have a large settlement, extending to the east and west of the fort. Recent excavations by Newcastle University and English Heritage have uncovered some of the stone foundations of the buildings, revealing a bathhouse that probably belongs to the fort, but may have been used by the civilian population. Most times, such as at Birdoswald and Corbridge, the settlements outlasted the military occupation of the fort. Indeed, Corbridge became a major Roman town (the only Roman town in northern England), with the fort being demolished and replaced with civic buildings.

There is also some evidence for Roman period tourism involving the Wall. Several Roman bowls and goblet-like objects have been found, which depict the Wall and include the names of the forts. These include the Rudge Cup, found in a well at a Roman villa, which names five forts in the western section of the Wall, a *patera* (a shallow bowl) discovered on the Staffordshire moorlands, which names four forts, and the Amiens skillet, found in France in 1949, which details six sites. Archaeologists have suggested that these are souvenirs of the Wall, where they may have been created and sold on to Roman citizens visiting Hadrian's Wall.

Religion

Religion features heavily in everyday life for the Romans, and it's no different on Hadrian's Wall. The evidence from numerous altars found at Roman sites is that many different gods were worshiped, from local deities such as Antenociticus, at Benwell, to Jupiter, the 'best and greatest god' as inscribed on several altars found at Maryport fort. There are several known (and quite a few suspected) temples found across Hadrian's Wall, including sites at Housesteads, Carrawburgh, Benwell and Maryport, with the latter site possibly having religious importance given the number of altars that have been recovered there. Christianity did not become the dominant religion until the beginning of the fifth century, with some evidence for its practice on the Wall coming from several possible early church buildings built at Housesteads and Birdoswald.

Although there was a lot of religious activity across the Wall, there are only two sites where there are significant remains of religious buildings which can be seen. The first, dedicated to the cult of Mithras, is on the western side of Carrawburgh fort. The temple is one of three known structures from the Wall, the others being outside the forts at Rudchester and Housesteads. Inscriptions mentioning the cult have also been at sites north of the Wall, High Rochester and Castlesteads, suggesting that there may be additional temples awaiting discovery.

Little is known about the cult, which is based on the classical story of Mithras, who captured a bull (a symbol of vitality), taking it back to his cave where he killed it, releasing the power of vitality, and it is this that the cult worshipers sought to invoke. It has its origins in Persia, but was quickly adopted by many in the army, who would build subterranean or partially submerged, darkened temples (to replicate the atmosphere of the original cave). They would also worship the sun god Sol, essentially celebrating light and darkness.

Great Chesters.

Another example of a surviving temple can be seen at Benwell on the edge of Newcastle. This temple was founded around AD 175 and, according to inscriptions found at the site, was dedicated to Antenociticus. The only mention of this deity anywhere in the Empire is at Benwell, so archaeologists think he may have been a local deity.

Although there are no remains to be seen, Maryport appears to have been a major religious centre, as seventeen altars have been found close to the fort in one small area. Although the site had been excavated previously, Newcastle University undertook a new programme of excavations in the early 2010s, not only discovering a new altar which the original excavators had missed but also conclude that there were two temples on site which were located in a specially created enclosure. It's likely that every fort on and around Hadrian's Wall had one or more temples in proximity, especially if there was a civilian settlement close by. The forts at Benwell, Birdoswald and Wallsend have all yielded evidence of temples in the local area, while artefacts found in and around the Wall also suggest there were many cults and religions being followed, something which is not unexpected given the diversity of those living on Hadrian's Wall.

Altar stones are the most prevalent sign of religion in the Roman, with hundreds of examples coming from the Wall and the supporting forts, and were an essential part of the worship of gods in the Roman period. Altars are square stone blocks, which range in size from a couple of metres to small 'portable' versions, which are less than 30 centimetres long (although still heavy objects to carry around). Altars are carved, with some having simple designs, while others can be more complex, and almost always there are inscriptions detailing which god the altar is dedicated to, who is doing the dedication and why. A particularly ornate example was found in the Mithraic temple at Carrawburgh, which is now at the Great North Museum in Newcastle, with a replica on display in the temple remains. The altar was dedicated to the sun god Sol and depicts the deity with rays of sun emanating from his head, but these have been cut through the rock, and there is a recess in the back enabling a candle to be placed in the back of the altar and lighting up the rays of sun. This would have been particularly effective in the darkened temple.

Roman altars would have looked very different to how they appear today. The Romans would have painted them bright colours, with the lettering often done in red, the background in white, and then the rest of the carvings individually painted. Ongoing research at Glasgow University has been using the latest scientific technology to identify the colours used on altars by analysing microscopic traces left on the stones. This research has been used by the Great North Museum to project the original colours onto some of the altar stones from the forts on Hadrian's Wall that are in their collection. On the top of the altar was a small dip or bowl carved into the surface where offerings would be made, a practice which seems to still be followed at Great Chesters fort where an altar stone has sat in the ruins of the south gate guard tower for over 100 years. Despite this not being the stone's original location (it probably came from either the headquarters building in the fort or somewhere in the surrounding settlement), and despite the stone being uninscribed and not dedicated to a particular deity, visitors continue to make offerings of coins to an unknown god.

There are many altars to be seen across the Wall and beyond, with the largest collections being in the museums at Maryport, Chesters, Housesteads, Birdoswald and Vindolanda, as well as Tullie House in Carlisle and the Great North Museum in Newcastle. There are also altars to be seen in the remains of the Mithraeum by

Carrawburgh fort, Lanercost Priory (where they were taken from Birdoswald fort), and even an example sitting outside of the church at Nether Denton, which itself is sited on top of one of the Stanegate forts.

Death

Death was, and still is, an inevitability of life, and the people living on and around Hadrian's Wall could not escape it. Human remains, including the occasional murder victim, have always been found around the Wall, and there are plenty of cemeteries by the forts and settlements. Scientific analysis of human remains can tell us much about that individual such as their age, sex, ethnicity, where they grew up, what sort of diet they had, and often how they died, although that type of analysis rarely tells us about the person – who they were and what they did in life. Instead, archaeologists look to grave markers or tombstones to learn more about the people who died on the Wall.

Tombstones have been frequently found along the Wall for centuries, and many examples of these can be seen in the museums at the forts, as well as at the Great North Museum and Tullie House. These often give us details about who the stone was for, who erected it, what their relationship was and occasionally how the individual died.

Tombstones are often ornately carved, depicting individuals in various poses, as well as having the inscription. Two such stones have been recovered from South Shields and can be seen in the fort museum. Both are ornately carved and depict figures in various poses and wearing certain fashions, from which archaeologists have been able to draw comparisons with Syrian culture, implying that the stonemason was probably from that part of the Roman Empire. Both tombs give an insight into life on the Wall, information we wouldn't otherwise know about. The first example is a memorial to a freed north African slave, Victor. It was commissioned by a cavalry soldier, Numerianus, who was Victor's former master. It's a touching reminder of how complex relationships, particularly with slaves (or former slaves), were in this period, particularly given the expense of such a tombstone. It is also a reminder that Hadrian's Wall was a mix of cultures, not just occupied by people from Rome. The other notable tombstone from South Shields was dedicated to the memory of Regina, another freed slave who was originally part of the Catuvellauni tribe based in southern England. She was the wife of Barates, who came from Syria, and it again demonstrates that the Wall became home to people from different cultures and vastly different parts of the Empire. We'll never know how or where the couple met, and what brought them to this remote frontier.

Another tombstone of note can be seen on display at Hexham Abbey, although where it originally stood is unknown. Dedicated to the memory of Flavinus, a Roman cavalry standard bearer, it was discovered in 1881 and at almost 3 metres tall; it is the largest tombstone known in Britain. The tombstone tells us that Flavinus died after seven years of service at the relatively young age of twenty-five, and depicts a high-ranking mounted soldier (possibly Flavinus) carrying a military standard and riding over a naked barbarian, which represents Roman subjugation of the indigenous tribes.

Few tombs or mausolea survive in Roman Britain, but there is a notable example from the northern outpost fort at High Rochester where the remains of a circular building can be seen. Located next to the remains of Dere Street as it approaches the fort on the south-east side, it survives several layers or courses high. The original building would probably have been shaped like a beehive and would have been around 5 metres high. It's unknown who occupied the tomb (if it was even a tomb), or how important they were.

Murder was not something unknown to the Wall communities, with several gruesome examples coming to light 1,900 years later. In the 1930s, a double grave was uncovered during excavations of the civil settlement outside the fort at Housesteads. One occupant of the grave, a man in his early forties, had the blade of a dagger sticking out of his rib cage, and would have broken off when the fatal blow was struck. In an even more gruesome twist, his companion may have been put in the grave after watching the first victim being stabbed. It's not clear how the companion died, or if they were still alive when placed into the shallow grave. Another grizzly find comes from Vindolanda fort. In 2010, the remains of a child, around eight to ten years old, was uncovered by volunteers excavating at the site. Subsequent analysis showed that the child was a long way from home having grown up in the Mediterranean. What was shocking about the discovery was that the child's skull had been crushed, although whether this was deliberate or accidental remains unclear, but either way, it ended their life. But what makes the death more suspicious is that the body was secretly buried under the floor of one building in the fort, something which was forbidden under Roman law.

Replica altars, Mithraeum at Carrawburgh.

4. Visiting Hadrian's Wall

Housesteads milecastle.

Hadrian's Wall is around 118 kilometres (74 miles) long and stretches across northern England from Wallsend (to the east of Newcastle) to Bowness (west of Carlisle), while there are additional forts along the coast of Cumbria, as well as to the north and south of the line of the Wall.

A Short Guide to Hadrian's Wall has been written to help visitors decide what they want to see and how to get there. Whether you're a casual day tripper, dedicating a few days to exploring the length of the Wall, or even just passing by on your way north or south, the *Short Guide* will have something for you.

Maps

Almost all the archaeological sites that are covered in this book are recorded on the Ordnance Survey (OS) Explorer maps and the official OSMaps app, with most appearing on the Landranger series. The line of the Wall and the *vallum* are also recorded on the OS maps, but in a few places this is speculative, and where possible this has been noted in the text. Most of the main sites are well signposted, especially from the Military Road (B6318), whereas only the major sites are signposted from the A69. Where possible, directions to access the archaeological sites have been included in the individual site descriptions, but it is recommended that visitors plan their visits especially as parking at many of the sites can be limited. The sites appear in an east to west order, but on occasions directions may differ to this to make it easier to visit the different sites.

Accessibility

Unfortunately, accessibility on and around Hadrian's Wall is very limited and will be difficult for those with limited mobility. Outside of the main attractions, there are few paved routes, and paths cut across fields that can frequently be muddy and wet. Most of these routes will involve using styles to cross over walls, passing through kissing gates, or using narrow planks to cross streams. In some places, footpaths past the Wall are less than a metre wide, and the archaeological remains can be an additional hazard, and at several sections, there are many steps or steep embankments to climb. Those sections of the Wall or forts which have no visitor facilities are the ones that are the least accessible.

The main forts are much more accessible, although the level of accessibility varies from site to site, with paths ranging from gravel to grass and mud tracks. While the paths can be accessible around the individual sites, the interiors of the forts tend to retain their original flooring and can be rocky and fragmented. The forts at Wallsend, South Shields, Vindolanda, Housesteads, Birdoswald and Carlisle Castle are the most accessible, although there are some steep hills on sites and not all parts of the site will be accessible for those with limited mobility. Accessible facilities such as toilets or access to cafés may also be limited at the various sites. The main museums off the Wall, Tullie House and the Great North Museum, are fully accessible. The main sites have accessibility statements available on their websites. Some notes regarding site accessibility have been included in the individual site descriptions produced here.

Transport

There are many ways to explore Hadrian's Wall – on foot, by train, bus or by car. The *Short Guide* is written with the latter in mind, although it will come in handy for anyone choosing another means to explore the area. Many of the sites featured here are easily accessed by foot and by car, although it is challenging to find parking for some of the more obscure parts of the Wall. Where possible, details of the best places to park have been included in the individual site descriptions. For the supporting forts, beyond the Wall, car is the easiest way to reach them as some of them are very rural. Pay and display ticketing is in operation in the main car parks, including those at most of the larger forts (Vindolanda has free parking), but the same ticket can be used at several car parks, so it is worth checking the situation at each site. There are limited opportunities to refuel and recharge vehicles on the line of the Wall itself, so it is worth planning ahead of a visit.

Bus and Trains

The best way to visit the Wall if not travelling by car is the AD122 bus (www.gonortheast.co.uk/ad122), which runs between Hexham and Haltwhistle daily (April to October), and weekends at other times of the year. Change at Haltwhistle for the 185 bus, which continues along the Wall as far as Birdoswald fort. Both bus routes stop at the main sites along the Wall, including Chesters, Housesteads, The Sill (for Cawfields Crags), and Vindolanda. It is possible to get a bus from Hexham and Haltwhistle to Carlisle (via Brampton) and then change for a service to Bowness-on-Solway or the Cumbrian coast. The route of the AD122 does occasionally change, so it is worth checking out the website for the latest updates. Be sure to get an AD122 Rover ticket, which gives unlimited travel on every bus route run by Go North East, while the tickets also give discounted entry to some of the sites.

The Tyne Valley Railway runs across northern England from Newcastle to Carlisle, stopping at several sites in-between (Corbridge, Hexham and Haltwhistle), and will often get you close to some of the main Roman sites, but inevitably you'll need to use local bus services to reach most sites. Trains also run from Carlisle down the Cumbrian coast to Barrow-in-Furness, stopping at Maryport, Workington and Whitehaven where there are Roman sites to be explored.

Walking the Wall

The *Short Guide* is aimed at those visiting individual sites on Hadrian's Wall along with the supporting forts, although there are several good guidebooks specifically focussed on

this aspect. Almost all of these books follow the Hadrian's Wall Path (which itself overlaps with the Pennine Way in the central section), a dedicated walker-friendly route which runs coast to coast for around 85 miles and is part of the National Trails network. The best times for walking the route is between May and October when the weather is slightly more favourable and the route is likely to be less wet and muddy. More information can be found on the National Trail website.

Hadrian's Wall is an ancient monument, protected by law, and at 1,900 years old, it is also quite fragile in places. Every year, teams of volunteers and professionals carry out numerous repairs on the Wall, forts and the footpaths and walkways along the Wall. This is partly because of erosion, but also because people clamber and walk on the ancient remains, so in recent years volunteers and the authorities have been campaigning to raise awareness of the damage that people are doing to the Wall, and are being encouraged to walk alongside the Wall and to stick to footpaths.

Accommodation

There are plenty of places to stay along and near to Hadrian's Wall and the supporting forts, particularly in Newcastle and Carlisle, but there are plenty of small hotels, bed and breakfasts and pubs on the line of the Wall. The local tourist information sites have more information on where to stay.

Countryside Code

Most sites covered in the *Short Guide* can be accessed by visitors, but there are a number that are privately owned – where possible, this has been stated in the individual site entries. For those sites that it is not possible to visit, if there is a nearby path or viewpoint from which the site can be seen, this has also been noted in the text. Most of the archaeological sites featured in the *Short Guide* are on agricultural land, and visitors are advised to check fields for livestock before accessing them, particularly if you have dogs with you.

In England, the Countryside Code (www.gov.uk/government/publications/the-countryside-code) applies to the landscape around Hadrian's Wall, and recommends the following for visitors:

- Consideration for those living and working in or enjoying the countryside.
- Leaving gates and property as you find them.
- Not blocking access to gateways and driveways.
- Follow local signs and keep to marked paths.
- Taking litter home.
- Not lighting fires.
- Keep dogs under control.
- Bag and bin dog poo.
- Check local conditions and plan your route.

In Scotland, all sites are accessible under the right to roam. The advice given to visitors as part of the Scottish Outdoor Access Code is similar to the Countryside Code and can be found at www.outdooraccess-scotland.scot

Dogs

Dogs are allowed at most sites on Hadrian's Wall, the exception being the museums and Vindolanda where they are not permitted on site. It is worth checking individual fort websites for information on access for those with dogs. By law in the UK, assistance dogs are allowed access to all sites and museums.

Finding Something Roman

If you've found an object that could be Roman, then there are several things you should do. Note the National Grid Reference (using at least six digits) and location where the object was found, handle it with care and don't clean it. Take photos of the object and its location, and try to avoid touching the ground where it was found in case archaeologists want to excavate. Then contact the local Finds Liaison Officer (www.finds.org.uk/contacts), who will advise you on what to do next. In Scotland, follow the steps above and contact the Treasure Trove Panel (www.treasuretrovescotland.co.uk).

It is important to understand that it is illegal to dig or metal-detect on a site that is legally protected as a scheduled monument – this includes all parts of Hadrian's Wall (including the fortifications), as well as the supporting forts and other Roman structures. Failing to declare found objects to the Portable Antiquities Scheme can be a criminal offence, so it is always best to check with the local Finds Liaison Officer, who will be happy to help. A range of guides and publications aimed at supporting anyone undertaking field walking, metal-detecting and mudlarking can be found at www.finds.org.uk.

5. The Sites

Gatehouse, South Shields.

This part of the *Short Guide* details the individual sites along Hadrian's Wall, as well as the supporting forts and is split into five parts, each covering different geographical sections: East (Wallsend to Corbridge/Hexham), Centre (Chesters to Great Chesters/Epiacum), West (Carvoran to Bowness-on-Solway), the Cumbrian coast (Kirkbride to Ravenglass), and the Outpost forts (Risingham, High Rochester, Bewcastle, Netherby and Birrens). Where known, the original names given by the Romans to the forts are included in each entry, along with the English translation. Some of the forts operate seasonal hours and may be closed in the winter.

Each entry follows the same format:

- Name
- Latin name (English translation when known)
- Site type, facilities, parking, entry charge (if not free)
- Website

- National Grid Reference | Postcode | What 3 Words
- An overview of the site with details of which features to see.
- Directions to the site

The National Grid Reference and What 3 Words location details are the most accurate locators as the postcodes defer to the nearest house or settlement, which can be some distance from the Roman site. The abbreviations used in the individual site listings: MC – Milecastle | MF – Milefortlet | T – Turret

Sources

A list of sources used for each individual site entry can be found in the Finding Out More section at the end of the *Short Guide.*

A Short Glossary of Terms

Antonine Wall	Built in AD 140, the Emperor Antoninus Pius, Hadrian's successor, built this Wall across central Scotland.
Aqueduct	A small channel used to bring water to forts, towns and buildings such as bathhouses. On Hadrian's Wall, these are cut into the ground or bedrock and covered with stone.
Artefacts	Objects or remains that help archaeologists tell the story of a site.
Auxilia	Auxiliary soldiers who patrolled the Wall and garrisoned the forts. Paid mercenaries recruited from around the Empire and who did not have Roman citizenship.
Barracks	Accommodation blocks for soldiers within the forts.
Berm	The space between the Wall and the *vallum.*
Broad Wall	The original curtain wall, which was reduced in thickness partway through construction and replaced by the Narrow Wall.
Cavalry	Horse riding soldiers.
Cohors	A unit or cohort of soldiers.
Courses	The layers of remaining stones forming part of the walls of a fortification, or Hadrian's Wall itself.
Crenellation	A defensive feature, often found on top of battlements, and is a stone, turf or wood barrier running the top of the structure, with regular gaps for firing projectiles such as arrows through. Some scholars speculate that there were crenellation along the top of Hadrian's Wall, although there is no evidence to support this.
Culvert	A drainage channel running through the Wall.
Curtain Wall	The stone or turf barrier.
Ditch	Part of the forward defences, running for most of the length of the Wall.

Earthworks	Lumps and bumps in the ground caused by physical remains beneath the surface.
Enclosure	An area secured by a wall or similar physical boundary.
Epigraphy	The study of inscriptions.
Excavation	The archaeological process of uncovering a buried historical site.
Finds	See artefacts.
Fort	A local base for infantry and/or cavalry soldiers varying in size, with administrative and headquarter functions. Early forts (particularly those on the Stanegate) were built with turf ramparts and had timber buildings on top of turf foundations, before being replaced with stone defences and internal structures.
Fortlet	Small fortification usually housing a small unit of soldiers and with a specific guarding function. In the west, these were built from turf before being replaced in stone.
Fortress	A base for legionary soldiers (i.e. York, Chester).
Horrea	Latin name for granaries, buildings for storing grain in the forts.
Indigenous	The people who were originally born and occupied Britain before the Romans arrived.
Infantry	Foot soldiers.
Legionaries	Soldiers officially based in legionary fortresses and constructed Hadrian's Wall.
Hypocaust	An underfloor heating system with distinct remains (a raised floor supported by small pillars). Usually found in bathhouses and the *praetorium* in forts.
Mansio	A type of government owned hotel, found outside some forts and which was used by officials on Imperial business.
Milecastle	A small fortlet positioned every mile or so between the forts of the Wall.
Milefortlet	Similar to a milecastle, but found between the forts on the Cumbrian coast as far south as Maryport.
Military Way	The road running between the curtain wall and the *vallum*.
Military Road	The eighteenth-century road running between Newcastle and Carlisle, partly constructed on top of the curtain wall.
Narrow Wall	A wall that replaced the Broad Wall and was thinner than it. It became the standard width for the curtain wall.
Praetorium	A courtyard-style building occupied by the commanding officer and their family within a fort.
Principia	The headquarters building in the centre of a fort, which had an administrative, religious and financial role.
Ramparts	The walls surrounding a fortification, which can either be built of turf or stone. Occasionally, the curtain wall is referred to as a rampart.
Roundhouse	The most common type of indigenous dwelling found in Iron Age Britain, with many continuing to be occupied during the Roman period.
Stanegate	The Roman road running between the forts at Corbridge and Carlisle.
Terminus	The end points of the Wall. At the eastern end this is the fort at Wallsend, and Bowness-on-Solway at the western end.
The Wall	Collective term used to refer to Hadrian's Wall – the curtain wall, the forward and rear defences and the fortifications.

Turf Wall	The curtain wall in the west, which was originally constructed from turf slabs (turves), but was replaced in stone around the same time as they replaced the Broad Wall with the Narrow Wall.
Turret	Guard towers for the Wall and on the Cumbrian coast, with two turrets every between the milecastles and milefortlets. In the west, these were timber before being replaced in stone and built into the Wall.
Vallum	The wide ditch, which runs for most of the length of the Wall and is part of the rear defences.

Hadrian's Wall: East

As part of the outer defences of Hadrian's Wall, the Romans built a fort at South Shields to protect the entrance to the River Tyne. But it is the fort on the northern side of the river, and a little further inland, which marks the eastern terminus of Hadrian's Wall. The river was a major supply route for the construction and ongoing occupation of the Wall, with building materials, goods, and even soldiers able to be brought far inland on the network of rivers running across the north of England. Sadly, mass industrialisation of the region around Newcastle from the seventeenth century onwards has led to the loss of many of the Roman remains in the area, including the Wall. It has only been in the past 100 years or so that archaeologists have begun to trace lost sections of Hadrian's Wall and rediscover lost Roman buildings as the old shipyards, docks and housing has been cleared away and the

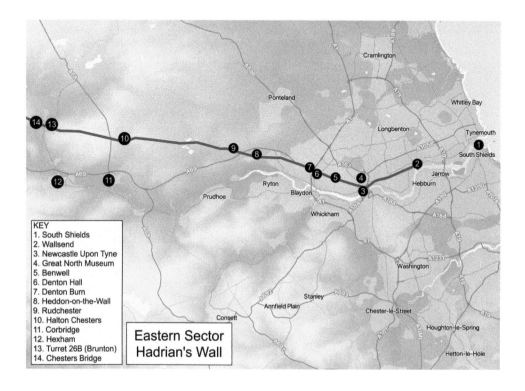

KEY
1. South Shields
2. Wallsend
3. Newcastle Upon Tyne
4. Great North Museum
5. Benwell
6. Denton Hall
7. Denton Burn
8. Heddon-on-the-Wall
9. Rudchester
10. Halton Chesters
11. Corbridge
12. Hexham
13. Turret 26B (Brunton)
14. Chesters Bridge

Eastern Sector
Hadrian's Wall

urban parts of the city redeveloped. From the plains around the mouth of the River Tyne, Hadrian's Wall makes its way through the suburbs of the city, parts of its original route now lost. From the neoclassical city centre, the Wall heads through the western suburbs, occasionally being glimpsed, before making its way through rolling countryside towards the hillier and more dramatic landscape of the central section.

South Shields
Arbeia (place of the Arabs)
Fort | Museum | Cafe (summer only) | Toilets | On Street Parking | Charge
arbeiaromanfort.org.uk
NZ 364 678 | NE33 2BB | parent.home.closes

Strategically positioned on a headland at the mouth of the River Tyne, the fort at South Shields not only had commanding views of the river and coast, but would have controlled access to this strategically important waterway, and to the eastern end of Hadrian's Wall. It was a site that continued to have strategic importance long after Hadrian's Wall was abandoned in favour of the Antonine Wall, with the fort taking on the role of a supply base for later northern campaigns. Recent research has suggested that the original name for the site was Lugudunum (fortress of the god Lugus), before it became better known as Arbeia in later years. At some point, the fort was the base for a unit of Tigris bargemen (the River Tigris flowing through Mesopotamia, which is modern Syria and Iraq), which shows the strategic importance of the River Tyne in the Roman period. Today, South Shields is home to some of the most impressive recreated Roman buildings anywhere in Britain.

Roman artefacts had, since at least the sixteenth century, been found around South Shields, and it was not until the Church of England sold off land for development, and the construction of new houses was underway, that the remains of the fort were uncovered. This attracted the attention of members of the nearby Society of Antiquaries of Newcastle upon Tyne who undertook a series of excavations revealing the full extent of the site. The building was stopped, although some of those houses which were already completed can still be seen on the north-eastern side of the site, and the fort site became the first archaeological park in Britain, known as the 'People's Roman Remains Park'. Preserving the site has allowed archaeologists to continue exploring and excavating at South Shields, and led to the construction of several replica buildings including the west gatehouse, a barrack building, and part of the commanding officers house.

Thanks to the antiquarians and public campaigners saving South Shields, it is a well-preserved site, and one that we know a lot about. With at least seven different periods of construction, the story of life at South Shields begins before the Romans. During excavation of the ground beneath the fort, archaeologists have uncovered evidence that the site was cultivated or farmed. Sometime between 400 and 100 BC, an indigenous dwelling, a roundhouse, occupied the site. By the end of 100 BC, the roundhouse had been burnt down, although the cause of the fire was not clear. Archaeologists also found some artefacts that indicated that there may have been a larger, pre-Roman settlement somewhere close to what would become the fort site, but which remains to be discovered.

Although a fort was established at nearby Newcastle by the mid-70s AD, the evidence from South Shields indicates that the earliest stone fort was only built there in the AD 160s, during the middle of the Antonine period. The Emperor Antoninus Pius would die in 161, and his Wall appears to have been abandoned shortly after. Archaeologists have speculated that an early turf and timber fort, possibly built during the reign of Hadrian or Antoninus

Pius, was constructed somewhere on the headland, as during excavations at the end of the twentieth century, a military parade ground (where soldiers practiced manoeuvres) was discovered underneath a later fort. Cutting through the parade ground was a defensive ditch from the stone fort, suggesting that the parade ground predated the fort, and must have belonged to an earlier Roman fortification. Eventually, the parade ground was covered over and timber buildings, probably from a settlement, were constructed on top of it, before these were demolished and the fort extended in the third century.

Additional work undertaken on the fort in the third century would see the site divided in two, with the southern half becoming a fort within a fort, while the northern half became a storage facility with thirteen granaries (forts usually have one). Soon after, the wall dividing the two sites was removed and another nine granaries were built, along with an additional barrack block. The large number of granaries were needed to sustain the forces of the Emperor Septimius Severus, who was campaigning in Scotland around 208–210. Grain would have been shipped from South Shields up the coast, supplying the fort at Cramond (just outside Edinburgh) on the Firth of Forth, as well as the large fortress, the main campaign headquarters, at Carpow on the Firth of Tay.

Around AD 300, fire destroyed the fort, although it is not clear if this was because of enemy action, an accident, or if it was a deliberate act by the military to clear the site before embarking upon another reconstruction. This 'new' fort made use of eight surviving granaries, converting them into barracks, and adding another two new barracks to the plan. A new courtyard house and headquarters were constructed on the site, and some archaeologists think this coincided with arrival of the Tigris bargemen. The fort continued to be occupied in the fourth and fifth centuries, with buildings demolished and new structures built in their place. There is some documentary evidence the fort site continued to be occupied long after the Romans had left Britain.

It's hard not to notice the Roman buildings that have recreated at South Shields, starting with the western gatehouse, which dominates the entrance to the site. Opened in 1981, it is built in the same location as the original gatehouse, with the defensive ditches, which surrounded every fort, restored. South Shields only had three ditches, but some forts had five or six. The ramparts, a series of steep embankments several metres high that separated the ditches, have not been recreated here. People arriving at the fort would have entered through one of the large entrances or portals in the gatehouse. In times of trouble, the large gates could be closed and would have withstood an attack from the most determined barbarians. The small windows, protected by wooden shutters, would have protected those inside from both the elements and enemy bombardment, but also creates a small, dark and almost claustrophobic interior. Today, the inside of the gatehouse is well lit, and the windows are glazed, making it a more enjoyable place to explore the displays of replica armour and the model of the fort, which details the layout of the site and how it originally looked.

From the top of the gatehouse, there is a good view of the fort, with the remains of different buildings that have been excavated over the years including several granaries (*horrea*), the commanding officers house (*praetorium*), barracks, some of the defensive walls which surrounded the site, and the northern gatehouse. As the fort was eventually converted into a supply base, the only known example of such a site in northern Britain, the layout is considerably different to all the other forts on Hadrian's Wall. Many of the visible remains date to different periods in the history of the site, which explains why there are two headquarter buildings (*principia*), one being part of the original fort and subsequently almost destroyed during remodelling, and other dating to a later period. The earlier headquarters building is on the north side of the site, next to the recreated barrack block and solely comprises a sunken room, the vault which housed the soldiers pay. Above this room, at ground level, would have been another space, a chapel which was home to the regimental standards, along with statues of the emperor and altars dedicated to certain deities. The gods would keep an eye on the valuables contained within. The later headquarters building can be seen towards the centre of the fort, and it is possible to climb down the steps into the original vault. The vaults are easy to recognise when exploring the remains of forts along Hadrian's Wall, and there are good examples, some of which still have some, or all of the original vaulted roofs intact, including at Chesters and Great Chesters.

At the southern end of the site are another series of reconstructed building: a barrack building and the commanding officer's house. The barracks show life for a Roman soldier, with conditions being quite cramped and smelly, with larger rooms at the end of the block for officers (these may have been better decorated to reflect the rank and social status of the officers). The rooms look a bit run down and damp, but the conditions are similar to those experiencing them 1,900 years ago. In one room there is a small hearth built against the wall, providing the only warmth and a means on which to cook food. In the cold and damp climate of northern England, soldiers must have spent a lot of time feeling cold. South Shields was also home to cavalry barracks, where soldiers would have slept in the same spaces as the animals. The barrack block was divided into double rooms, with horses stabled on the inside and soldiers in the rear room. Living side by side with the horses would have been an uncomfortable and smelly experience.

The reconstruction of the commanding officer's house shows life at the opposite end of the spectrum from the ordinary soldiers. The commander would have had slaves, been accompanied by his family, and even had a small Mediterranean-style garden at the centre of his home. The building comprises a series of spacious rooms surrounding a courtyard, although this is only a partial reconstruction of half of the house. On entering, the courtyard is on the right, and is a similar style to Roman houses found in central Italy. The walls were painted with bright colours and different images, often scenes from classical myths – these designs have been inspired from original Roman walls found by archaeologists from different sites around the Empire, including Pompeii. On the left are a series of rooms, the original function of which is not known, but these may have been function or social spaces, with furniture modelled on items found at sites like Pompeii and Herculaneum. At the opposite end of the building from the entrance is a large reception room, which was probably used for the commanding officer and his wife to meet important visitors to the fort, as well as for entertaining friends and relaxing. Before leaving the building, there are a wonderfully ornate set of doors at the far end of courtyard. Wooden doors have survived at some of the sites in Italy, and the recreation is a good example of the style of door that was probably found at South Shields.

Just outside the commanding officer's house, by the vault from old headquarters building, is a large raised, grassy area. Around 1.5 metres higher than the rest of the fort site, the space is the last remaining unexcavated area at South Shields. The depth shows the significant change in the surface level between the Roman period and now, and how much soil that archaeologists have to dig through when excavating sites in this part of the world. Even then they would come to the last fort that the Romans built, and would have to dig down even deeper to get to the earliest ground levels.

Some artefacts uncovered within the fort can be seen in the on-site museum at the main entrance, although there is a larger collection of finds from South Shields on display at the Great North Museum in Newcastle. The finds include a very rare example of Roman chain mail, which was found in officers' quarters within the barrack block. There are also several tombstones on display, including that of Regina, a freed slave who was from southern England and married to Barates from Palmyra in modern Syria. Interestingly, her face on the tombstone has been chipped away. A second tombstone in the museum is that of North African slave, Victor. The ornate and expensive memorial was commissioned by his former master, Numerianus, a cavalry soldier. Like Regina's tombstone, the face of Victor has also been vandalised. Both tombstones are a reminder that not only were slaves, and their freed equivalents, living on and around Hadrian's Wall, but the whole of the north of England was a multicultural environment, with indigenous tribespeople mixing with, and even marrying, people from other parts of the Empire, not just Syria and North Africa.

Directions & Accessibility: South Shields is a good place to begin your explorations of the eastern end of Hadrian's Wall, with Wallsend (Segedunum) fort, the eastern terminus of Hadrian's Wall, just a twenty-minute drive away through the Tyne Tunnel. South Shields itself is also worth exploring, with miles of sandy beaches to the east of the fort, although dogs can only access certain areas in the summer months. There are a range of seaside attractions, restaurants, amusements and fairground rides all within a ten-minute walk of the fort.

The fort itself does not have any parking, but there is on-street parking in the streets surrounding the fort, while there are several large car parks by the seashore, to the east of the fort, but these fill up quickly at busy times, and there is a ten-minute walk to the fort, up a hill. The site itself is fairly accessible, although the paths can be a little stony in places. Access to the upper floors of the gatehouse is via wooden steps (there is no lift), and the interior space is narrow in places.

South Shields.

Wallsend
Segedunum (strong fort)
Fort | Museum | Café | Toilets | Parking | Charge
www.segedunumromanfort.org.uk
NZ 301 660 | NE28 6HR | vibes.hang.frame

The fort at Wallsend marks either the beginning, or the end of Hadrian's Wall, depending on which direction it's being approached from. Often known by its Latin name, Segedunum, it is a well-preserved site with a good museum, which has a viewing tower giving great views of both the fort, the course of the Hadrian's Wall through the city to the east, and almost over to South Shields fort to the south-east. Wallsend also marks the beginning of the Hadrian's Wall National Trail, a walking route that stretches from the River Tyne to the Solway Firth and closely follows the line of the Wall. With a museum, shop, regular family-friendly activities, a viewing platform, and not forgetting the fort and bathhouse, Wallsend is the perfect place to start your explorations of the eastern end of Hadrian's Wall.

Unlike many sites on Hadrian's Wall, where there have been pockets of excavation, archaeologists have been able to uncover most of Wallsend fort after clearance of industrial buildings and housing on the site. The initial excavations took place over a decade from the mid-1970s, with subsequent investigations in the 1990s and more recently around 2014. The investigations in the 1990s were the beginning of an £8 million programme of investment in the site, creating an archaeological park, with the remains of the fort on display, establishing a modern museum and education centre, and building a replica of the bathhouse.

Like many other forts on and around Hadrian's Wall, archaeologists excavating below the fort have found evidence that before the Romans, the site was farmed, but this stopped, possibly at the behest of the Romans when they constructed the fortifications. Archaeologists believe Wallsend was one of the original Hadrian's Wall forts which was built in the early 120s. The archaeologists have discovered that the walls of the fort defences were built into Hadrian's Wall, meaning that they were both constructed at the same time. The internal buildings of the fort were a mixture of timber and stone, with barracks, which held up to 500 cavalry and infantry soldiers, built out of wood. The central range of buildings (the granaries, headquarters, and commanding officer's house) were built out of stone. During excavations, the archaeologists found some evidence that suggested there was a timber structure underneath the headquarters building, which could suggest an earlier Roman building.

The second century saw the barracks rebuilt in stone, and a new building, which archaeologists think was a hospital, was built next to the granaries. These buildings are often found in Roman forts from this time, and a good example can be seen at Housesteads. The fort was occupied throughout the Hadrianic period and into the Antonine one, with more timber buildings replaced with stone in this period, along with refurbishment of other buildings. Defences around the fort were enhanced in the third century with an extra ditch added, but seemingly not around the whole of the fort. Around this time, there is evidence that some archaeologists think indicate that a market may have regularly been held in the fort. This is perhaps unsurprising, given that there was a settlement surrounding the fort on the south and west side, although this was abandoned by the late third century.

Evidence from pottery found during excavations suggests that there was a North African presence at the site. It's not clear if the pottery arrived at Wallsend through trade or was made by North African potters who had migrated to the region. The other explanation is that North African soldiers were stationed on the Wall. By the fourth century, defensive ditches had been filled in, and a new single, wider ditch dug to surround the site, while inside the fort there was extensive remodelling. After this time, less is known about the fort because of modern agricultural works and later building construction has destroyed evidence of later Roman activity.

The museum has a good collection of Roman objects, with plenty for families to see and do, with regular events taking place. On the ground floor is the shop and the Roman Gallery, with an interesting film about the fort and this part of Hadrian's Wall. There are various artefacts on display, with more to be seen in the Great North Museum in Newcastle. Have a look for the fragments of roof tile with a cat paw print or a child's footprint on them. There is also a collection of teeth from a four-year-old child, which were found buried underneath a building from the nearby civilian settlement. While in the Roman Gallery, look out for the stone toilet seats – chilly to use in the colder months. On the second floor is the café and exhibition spaces, one focussing on Roman history and the other celebrating the shipbuilding heritage of Wallsend. Don't forget to visit the viewing tower on the upper level. Accessible by lift, there are cracking views of the surrounding area. From the museum, the fort site is accessed by following the path, and is signposted with explanations of the different buildings that can be seen.

In the south-western corner of the fort is a replica Roman bathhouse, but based on the remains found at Chesters Roman fort because until recently the original bathhouse for Wallsend fort was lost under urban development. Luckily, the replica is very similar to the remains found nearby, but unfortunately the building is permanently closed to visitors because of issues with the safety of the structure. The website will contain the latest information if this changes. During excavation of the site before the replica bathhouse was built, there was a gruesome discovery as archaeologists uncovered the remains of the head of a child in the foundations of a Roman building. There was an absence of other bodily remains, leading archaeologists to conclude that someone deliberately buried the head when the original building was being constructed.

Just a few minutes' walk away, on Buddle Street, and on the line of the original, is a recreated section of Hadrian's Wall. The section is one interpretation of what Hadrian's Wall may have looked like, and has a walkway along the top, along with crenellations (gaps in the battlements for arrows to be fired through), although there is no archaeological evidence to support either of these features on the Wall. Set in a small enclosed park, it is part of the museum and a ticket is needed for entry. However, the section of wall is visible from the adjacent street.

The most recent discovery at Wallsend is the original bathhouse, which was built and used by soldiers from the fort. It was discovered in 2014 when the area to the south-west of the fort, formerly occupied by the Ship Inn, was being cleared. Lying 130 metres from the gates of the fort, the bathhouse was a massive 3.75 metres beneath modern ground level. An aqueduct brought water from north of the Wall, and supplied the bathhouse, which it is located so far from the fort. The bathhouse is similar in design to other such buildings on Hadrian's Wall, although at some point part of the building was abandoned and the rest of it remodelled to create a smaller bathhouse. Archaeologists have suggested that this was because the land the bathhouse was built on was unstable, some walls splitting away from the main structure and slipping towards the river. Efforts to shore up the walls by building buttresses against the outside walls had limited success.

To reach the bathhouse from the fort car park, head towards the river and pass through the gate onto the old railway line path. Almost directly opposite the gate, and in the grounds of an old factory, is a section of Roman stonework. This is the last visible section of Hadrian's Wall, which ran from the corner of Wallsend fort for about 180 metres to the edge of the River Tyne, although archaeologists have speculated that it may have jutted out into the river to form a pier or monumental structure designed to impress visitors arriving at Hadrian's Wall by sea. Continue west along the path and turn left after passing the replica bathhouse. The new bathhouse is well signposted, and only a few minutes' walk away. The excavated remains are visible from ground level and interpretation panels give a history of the bathhouse and its recent discovery. Only part of the bathhouse has been excavated and is on display, with the building likely to be much larger and still hidden under the surrounding roads.

Directions & Accessibility: Located to the east of Newcastle city centre, in the suburb of Wallsend, the site is signposted from all the major roads in the area, and is easy to find, especially if coming from South Shields on the south side of the River Tyne.

The site is accessible, with good paths around most of the remains. The museum is fully accessible with lifts to reach the upper levels, including the viewing tower. There is parking on site, although there are plans to redevelop parts of the site, including the car park, but there is on street parking in the areas around the fort. It is also possible to park next to the remains of the bathhouse, which is to the south-west of the fort site. Local residents can get reduced entry to the site. The website has information on this, as well as the ongoing developments at Wallsend fort.

Wallsend.

**

Between the forts of Wallsend and Newcastle, there are no visible remains of Hadrian's Wall or any of the associated structures. From time to time, pockets of Wall foundations are uncovered during road or building works. The Wall seems to have roughly followed what is now Fossway and Shields Road, although the crossing point of the Wall over the River Ouseburn is unknown. A walk from Newcastle city centre, along the River Tyne and up the first mile or so of the River Ouseburn, taking in a few of the riverside pubs on the way, and then back to the city centre following the projected line of the Wall, is a good way to explore this section. Additional foundations of the Wall have been located by Stepney Bank, Crawhill Road, south of St Dominic's Church, Gibson Street, Grenville Terrace, Jubilee Road and Garth's Head, before the Wall heads towards the fort now underneath Newcastle Castle.

**

Newcastle Upon Tyne
Pons Aelii/Aelius (Aelian Bridge)
Fort | No facilities | No Parking
NZ 250 638 | NE1 1RN | tonic.tribune.gains

Guarding a major crossing point over the River Tyne, the fort is named after the Roman bridge that once stood here – *pons* means 'bridge' in Latin, while *Aelii* comes from *Aelius*, the family name of the Emperor Hadrian. The fort was on a slight outcrop, but now lies underneath Newcastle Castle and the modern city, although there are a couple of glimpses of Roman life if you know where to look.

There is some possibility of Roman activity in the area from around the AD 120s, although this is based on altars recovered from close to the River Tyne and is debated by archaeologists. The fort itself was not built until the end of the second or early third century, with some evidence of activity on the site in the fourth century. Our knowledge of Roman activity in this part of the city is sketchy, although we have a growing picture of the military activity usually because of modern development and construction – we know the Black Gate sits on top of the north gate of the fort, while the southern defences extended as far as the Bridge Hotel, while part of the forts headquarters building and commanding officer's accommodation lie underneath the castle keep, which used Roman stone from the fort in its construction. There is some indication that the site continued to be occupied after the Romans had long disappeared from Britain, with establishment of an Anglo-Saxon cemetery on the fort site. Some archaeologists argue that there is likely to be a long-lost minster or early church somewhere in the immediate area, a tradition continued by Newcastle Cathedral, which occupies the north-east corner of the fort site. Like most other forts associated with Hadrian's Wall, there seems to have been a settlement surrounding the fort. Although the size and extent of this is unknown, its existence was confirmed during development work to the west of the fort. The location of the original Roman bridge is lost, but there is speculation that it lies somewhere in the vicinity of the swing bridge, which sits in the shadow of its better-known counterpart, the Tyne Bridge.

Directions & Accessibility: The fort at Newcastle lies more or less beneath the castle, the keep and a bridge. The castle is signposted from the city centre, and is to the east of Newcastle Central station. There are few surviving remains of the fort to be seen, with those visible including small sections of the granary, headquarters building, and commanding officer's house, all of which are visible underneath the arches of the adjacent rail bridge and free to access. There is limited on-site interpretation of the fort, and the remains give the appearance of being neglected.

Operating on seasonal hours, Newcastle Castle (www.newcastlecastle.co.uk) is open to the public, although there is limited mention of the Roman history of the site. The best-preserved section of the medieval town wall at West Walls is only a fifteen-minute walk from Newcastle Central station – from there, cross the road and go along Pink Lane, cross over Clayton Street West, continuing on Pink Lane and then cross Westgate Road to West Walls. Durham Tower is the first visible tower, in the centre of West Walls, with Herber Tower at opposite far end of the street. Following the line of the path to the right is Mordern Tower, an occasional venue for cultural events, and then Ever Tower is at the end. Turn right and head back along Stowell Street, through the heart of Newcastle's China Town, and two thirds of the way along the road, on your left is a building with a Norman-style arch and Dispensary Lane, which takes you to a hidden medieval gem of the city, the remains of Blackfriars, a thirteenth-century friary. Home to the Dominican order of monks, the friary was dissolved in 1539 and the land subsequently sold the town council and became home to the craft guilds, ensuring preservation of the cloisters and several surviving buildings that can be seen today. The site is open to visitors and is also home to the Blackfriars Restaurant, which runs regular medieval dining themed events in the old buildings of the friary.

**

From the fort at Newcastle Castle, the line of the Wall runs parallel with Westgate Road, albeit a little to the south before reaching Benwell.

**

Great North Museum: Hancock (Newcastle upon Tyne)
Museum | Café | Toilets | Free
www.greatnorthmuseum.org.uk
NZ 248 651 | NE2 4PT | miss.punks.offers

The largest museum in the north-east of England, the Hancock as it's known locally, houses a substantial collection of Roman artefacts and objects gathered from sites along Hadrian's Wall, as well as sites across the north of England by the Society of Antiquaries of Newcastle upon Tyne. Highlights include a model of Hadrian's Wall, which snakes its way across the ground floor of the museum, a recreation of the temple of Mithras from Carrawburgh fort, a large collection of tombstones and altars, domestic items including pottery and jewellery, and a range of military objects including original Roman armour and weapons.

The Hancock has much more to offer than just the Roman collections, and also has extensive natural and local history collections, with many objects from before and after the Romans including Bronze Age swords and weapons, several important Anglo-Saxon sculptures, several Egyptian artefacts including mummies, and an extensive collection of medieval objects mainly recovered from around the city. Besides objects from north-east England, there is also a collection of artefacts from excavations in Palestine in the 1930s and South America.

With regular events for families and adults, a visit to the Hancock can take up the best part of a day, while the remains of Newcastle Castle and the adjacent Roman fort are close by and also worth visiting. The Hancock is widely accessible, with a range of facilities including a cloakroom and café, although there is no dedicated parking, but there are multistorey car parks a few minutes' walk away.

Directions & Accessibility: Newcastle Central station is about a thirty-minute walk from the museum, with the nearest Metro station being Haymarket.

Benwell
Condercum (place with a wide view)
Fort | Temple | Vallum Crossing | No Facilities | On Street Parking
www.english-heritage.org.uk
Temple: NZ 217 646 | NE15 6QP | score.vague.takes
Vallum Crossing: NZ 215 646 | NE15 6QH | pines.woods.weep

Benwell is the first place, after Wallsend, where there are visible Roman remains. Although the fort and the Wall remains hidden under urban development, a small section of the *vallum*, the wide ditch which runs to the south of the Wall, can be seen, along with the remains of a temple.

Known in Latin as the place with a wide view, it is not surprising that the Romans chose this location for their fort given the sweeping views to the south, which can still be glimpsed between the houses that now surround most of the area. site. The fort, which originally would have sat astride West Road, has long since disappeared, with the north half destroyed during construction of a reservoir in the nineteenth century, while the southern half has been covered over by houses and industrial units in the early part of the twentieth century. Long before the fort was demolished, antiquarians recorded much of what was later to be destroyed, although subsequent and more recent excavations during redevelopment of the Benwell area have added to knowledge of the site. Recent work has shown that much of the fort survives beneath the ground, with some bits of the fort barely 40 centimetres underneath the modern surface.

Occupied for most of its history by the *ala I Asturum*, a cavalry regiment, the fort had the same layout as others on Hadrian's Wall, although the strong room in the headquarters building was carved out of rock. Like Wallsend fort, there was also evidence of a hospital building in the central range, along with a workshop and another building that had an unknown purpose. Lumps of coal were discovered in the fort workshop, and with coal seams near the surface in the Benwell area, archaeologists think the Romans may have used it as part of their industrial workings. The bathhouse, which was discovered and recorded before being destroyed in the 1750s, was located to the south-west of the fort. It shared a design with many other bathhouses on Hadrian's Wall.

A large civilian settlement surrounded the fort on the west, east and south sides. Recent excavations have found evidence of stone buildings in the settlement, which has yielded evidence of occupation in the second and third centuries. Archaeologists noted that some of the stone buildings were built to a high standard for a Wall fort settlement. They also found the remains of a building that they thought was a warehouse. To the north of the fort, beyond the Wall, archaeologists also made some interesting discoveries, with evidence for a road leaving the fort, heading north through land which had originally been cultivated. They also found evidence of industrial activity in the area, which appeared to be contemporary with Roman activity in the area, but took place beyond the safety of the Wall. All the evidence seems to suggest that Benwell, and the surrounding settlement, was an important and prosperous place in the past.

To the south-east of the fort are the remains of the temple, which was discovered in 1862. Several altars were found at the site, and from inscriptions found on these, the temple was dedicated to Antenociticus, probably a local deity as this is the only site in the Empire where there are dedications to him. A statue head, recovered from the temple remains, and which can be seen in the Great North Museum, is believed to be of Antenociticus. When the site was discovered, the walls had collapsed, and among the rubble were burnt timbers and roof tiles. This has led some archaeologists to speculate that the temple may have been burnt down by angry Christians or enemy action. After the destruction of the temple, the site was used as a cemetery, with three graves found within the remains. It may not have been the only temple in the area, as additional artefacts have been in the area, which suggest there may have been another temple or temples nearby.

The *vallum* at Benwell diverts to the south of the fort, and there was a crossing over the ditch, a road enabling access to the fortification and the Wall beyond it. On top of the road over the *vallum* crossing was a large set of gates, designed to control access to the fort and Wall, and protect a weak point in the Wall defences. To give the soldiers manning the gate more control over traffic flow, the gates opened inwards. Benwell is the only point on the Wall where the remains of a *vallum* crossing and its gate can be seen.

Directions & Accessibility: There are no visible remains of the fort at Benwell, but the temple and the vallum crossing are worth looking at. Both are within a short distance of each other. Coming from the direction of Newcastle city centre, it's easiest to begin with the temple site, located at the north end of Broomridge Avenue, just off West Road. Set in among a housing estate, the open-access site is set in a small grassed area between two houses. As well as the remains of the temple building, there are several replica altars inside. There is no formal path around the site, and the gate may not be wide enough for some wheelchair users, but the site is visible from the pavement.

To see the vallum crossing, head onto West Road from the temple site and turn left, taking the first left into Denhill Park. The vallum crossing is at the southern end of this small housing estate. The area is fenced in and usually locked, but the crossing can be seen through the railings from the pavement, with the large blocks which supported the gate still visible.

Roman temple, Benwell.

**

From Benwell, the next set of visible remains are at Denton, a short drive to the west. Heading along West Mains Road, the first fragment of the Wall can be seen in the forecourt of the petrol station at the roundabout at West Road/Denton Road (A191). It's a small section, about a metre long, and is behind the forecourt sign, next to the old adjoining building. More significant are the remains a little further on, past the roundabout and still on the southern side of the dual carriageway. Excavated in 1927, archaeologists have speculated that this stretch of Wall would have been at least 2.75 metres wide at this point. There is no parking on West Road itself, but there is parking at Denton Burn Library, and this section of Wall is next to this and visible from the main road. From here continue on West Road to Denton turret.

**

Denton Hall
Wall | Turret | No Facilities | On Street Parking
www.english-heritage.org.uk
Turret T7b (Denton Hall): NZ 198 655 | NE15 7TE | mile.buck.update

Denton Hall, on the outskirts of Newcastle, is the location of the first stretch of Wall that also has the visible remains of a turret. Originally excavated in 1929, the nearby Wall was further investigated in the late 1980s during development work for the A1. Inside the turret, there are the remains of a platform for steps or a ladder leading to the upper level of the building, and possibly onto the Wall, enabling soldiers to patrol and monitor anyone approaching from the north or south.

Directions & Accessibility: The stretch of Wall and the turret at Denton Hall are next to West Road. They are easy to visit; although there is no parking on West Road, there is on street parking on Turret Road on the south side of the Wall. Heading west from Newcastle city centre on West Road, take a left onto Broadwood just after Denton Burn library, then take the first right onto Turret Road. The section of Wall is on the right after about 80 metres.

The site is grassed with no paths and surrounded by a low (30 cm) railing, which can be crossed to access the interior of the turret, where there is an interpretation panel. The site can be easily seen from the adjacent pavement.

Denton Burn
Wall | *Vallum* | No Facilities | On Street Parking
www.english-heritage.org.uk
Wall: NZ 195 656 |NE5 2BN | glow.agreed.sports
Vallum (Denton Burn): NZ 194 655 | NE15 7RE | hogs.tests.priced

The remains at Denton are divided by the A1, which cuts through the Wall as it heads north. On the western side of the A1, on the line of the A69, there is a low-lying stretch of Wall, which runs alongside the southern carriageway of the road. A couple of streets to the south of this stretch of Wall, the first visible remains of the *vallum* can be seen in the middle of a housing estate. Although these are not the most impressive remains of the *vallum*, having been eroded by agriculture and development over the centuries, they indicate how formidable this earthwork must have once been.

Hadrian's Wall, Denton Burn.

Directions & Accessibility: To visit the section of Wall and vallum at Denton Burn, cross over the A1 from Denton Hall, following the A69. Take the first left onto Southway, and a left again onto The Rampart, where you can park next to the Wall.

To visit the vallum, go back onto Southway and take a left, then take the second right. The large grassy area on the left, with a gentle slope and ditch, are the remains of the vallum.

* *

Heading westwards, from Denton, there are few opportunities to see sections of the Wall and its defences until you get closer to Heddon-on-the-Wall. If you want to follow the line of the Wall, head west on the A69 from Denton, and turn off at the first exit signposted Walbottle (B6528). If you are aiming to visit the sites on the central or western sections of the Wall, it is quicker to stay on the A69 and follow the signs marked with the brown Roman helmet.

The B6258 (Hexham Road), mostly, follows the line of Hadrian's Wall. In places, the road sits on top of the foundations of the Wall, while the vallum runs parallel to the south. Although there are few physical remains to be seen before Heddon, there are some small earthworks indicating the original location of some of the minor fortifications on the Wall. Continue through Throckley, where the Wall and vallum are under housing, and continue towards Heddon. Just before entering the village, as the road heads down a slope, the remains of the Wall can be seen on the left-hand side.

* *

Heddon-on-the-Wall
Wall | No Facilities | On Street Parking
www.english-heritage.org.uk
NZ 136 669 | NE15 0DU | loaded.likely.idea

Heddon is home to the first lengthy, surviving section of Hadrian's Wall, and one which is easy to visit and explore. The section of Wall visible here is the Broad Wall, which survives up to seven courses high in places, while in fields to the south of the Wall, it's possible to make out some of the southern defences, including the north mound and *vallum*, although this can be difficult to see when the vegetation is high. In 2018, archaeologists undertook a geophysical survey at Heddon, and discovered a series of pits on the north side of the Wall, although it's not possible to see these on the ground today. Arranged in a regular pattern, archaeologists believe these were an extra layer of defence against attacking enemies, with the pits being filled with spikey vegetation or sharpened sticks. Recent excavations from elsewhere in the eastern section of the Wall (by Wallsend and Byker in the Newcastle suburbs) have also led to the discovery of these pits, which were probably a common defensive feature for the Wall, although there is no evidence for these in the central and western sections but this could be because, in the past, archaeologists were not aware of these and missed them during excavations.

Directions & Accessibility: If approaching from the A69, take the exit marked Heddon-on-the-Wall, and take the first left past the village sign, then the first right into the village. If coming from Throckley, take the first left into the village. The path for Hadrian's Wall is on the left on the corner, through the hedge. There is no dedicated parking in Heddon, but it is possible to park in the village. There is no formal path alongside the Wall, although the ground is grassed and bumpy in places. The village is small but interesting to explore, especially the area around the church, as well as Wylam brewery, which has its home in the village.

Heddon-on-the-Wall.

Rudchester
Vindobala/Vindovala (white peak/white walls)
Fort | No Access
rudchester.org
NZ 112 675 | NE15 0JA | volume.replaying.shoelaces

Housing a mixture of around 500 infantry and cavalry soldiers, Rudchester fort survived as late as the eighteenth century when the stonework was removed for building field boundaries and agricultural buildings. Only a few small earthworks are now visible at the site, which remains in private hands and is not open to visitors.

The fort has only been examined a few times, and despite the lack of building remains, there have been several important artefacts recovered from the site including remains of the fort, but important finds have come from the site, including a life-size statue of Hercules, which is now in the collection of the Great North Museum in Newcastle. Rudchester is also one of the few fort sites on Hadrian's Wall where a Mithraic temple has been discovered close by, the others being Carrawburgh and Housesteads. In the 1840s, five altars dedicated to Mithras were recovered from the site, which was subsequently extensively excavated in 1953. Evidence from the excavations indicates the temple was not built until the end of the second century, or possibly even at the beginning of the third, but lasted until the fourth century. Underneath the temple was evidence of earlier buildings, although it is not clear if these were temples or something else.

Geophysical surveys in the 1990s indicated that there was a settlement on the south and probably on the west side of the fort. Although there has been no further investigative work, this and the extent or type of buildings in the settlement are unknown. Geophysical survey also identified the course of the *vallum*, which originally ran to the south of the fort, showing that it was already under construction before the Romans built the fort here.

Another curious feature near Rudchester is the Giants Grave, which is as morbid as it first sounds. It is a recess cut into the rock on the west side of the modern farm. Archaeologists believe that this was originally a water cistern which stored and supplied water to the fort. However, when it was first discovered and cleared in the eighteenth century, the grizzly remains of human bones were uncovered along with a candlestick. It is not known how the occupant, who was not a giant, died or whether they were placed in the Grave before or after dying.

Directions & Accessibility: There are no standing features to be seen at the site, except the fort platform. The fort itself is divided in two by the Military Road (B6318), which cuts through the middle of the fort. The fort itself is in private ownership and access is limited, but it is possible to park in a small layby, just past the farm entrance.

Halton Chesters
Onnum (stream)
Fort | No Access
NY 997 684 | NE45 5PZ | lilac.laminate.label

Cutting through the centre of Halton Chesters fort, the modern road follows the line of the Roman road that originally ran through the centre of the fort. Archaeologists believe that the Wall and ditch were built before the fort was added at a later date. Originally constructed early in the second century, the fort was rebuilt the following century, along

Halton Chesters.

with a secure enclosure that was attached to the south-west side of the fort. Known as an annexe, these enclosures are rare on forts in the north of England, and are more commonly found on sites in Scotland.

   Excavations at Halton Chesters took place in the 1930s, and again between 1956 and 1961. More recently, the fort and the surrounding area have been geophysically surveyed. The results have revealed many of the internal buildings, including barracks and a bathhouse in the northern half of the site, along with a granary in the southern section. Evidence from the granary showed two phases of the building, with the first being destroyed by fire around the turn of the second century. During excavation of the east gate, archaeologists found the pivot hole, the socket which supports the gate to turn, was badly worn. Those on the western side were unworn, indicating that these gates had been blocked up and remained unused. The gatehouse was also where an inscription dedicated to the Emperor Hadrian by the Sixth Legion was found face down in the ground. Geophysical survey has led to the discovery of several buildings outside of the fort, which are likely to belong to the settlement, while there is also evidence for cultivation of the surrounding area in the Roman period.

Directions & Accessibility: The Military Road (B6318) cuts through the centre of the fort at Halton Chesters, and there are no upstanding remains to be seen. On the south side of the road are some minor earthworks which show where some of the internal buildings of the fort were located. The fort itself is on private land and there is no direct access to the site and no parking nearby.

Corbridge
Corstopitum (place of the small birch trees)
Fort | Town | Museum | Toilets | Parking | Charge
www.english-heritage.org.uk
Fort & Town: NY 981 648 | NE45 5NT | banter.stole.chestnuts
Bridge: NY 983 644 | NE45 5NT | embraced.prouder.grounding

Corbridge Roman town is one of the most impressive archaeological sites in northern England, if not the UK, with extensive surviving remains indicating clearly what the site used to look like. The opportunity to wonder around an original Roman town, the most northerly in Britain, is not to be missed. The site also contains one of the best museums on Hadrian's Wall, which contains many of the artefacts on site, and gives a real glimpse into military and civilian life on Rome's most northerly frontier.

Located on Dere Street, the main Roman road from the legionary fortress at York to Scotland, Corbridge is the eastern terminus of the Stanegate, although some archaeologists believe that road continued further east. Roman remains here have been known about for centuries, with records of King John sending men here to seek treasure in the 1200s, while in the seventeenth and eighteenth centuries antiquarians recorded the ruins. Sadly, many of these were subsequently destroyed due because of agricultural works early in the nineteenth century. The first explorations at Corbridge took place in the 1860s, but it was not until the early twentieth century that extensive excavations took place, with the remains uncovered during those works now visible at the site. Most recently, the area around the Roman town has been surveyed by archaeologists from Newcastle University, revealing the extent of the settlement, along with agricultural systems, cremations, and even a mausoleum. The remains on display at Corbridge today show only part of the town, with more buildings beneath the surrounding fields.

Before the town, the Roman military established a fort at Corbridge, with an early single ditched enclosure being built a little way from the site of the Roman town. Occupation began in the AD 70s, lasting for a maximum of twenty years before it was abandoned and a new fort constructed on the site of what is now the Roman town. That fort was eventually burnt down and a new one was built on the site, which was then rebuilt around the same time as Hadrian's Wall was constructed, but occupation was brief and it seems to have been rebuilt around the time that the Antonine Wall was built in the 140s. The central fort buildings were constructed out of stone or timber on stone foundations, and the barracks in timber. The remains of the fort headquarters building can still be seen within the large Imperial building in the town. After this fort was demolished, there was another fort built on the site, which was abandoned in the latter half of the second century. The rebuilding of so many forts on top of each other is not unusual, with some of the Hadrian's Wall forts being rebuilt and remodelled into numerous fortifications.

Around AD 160, Corbridge became home to legionary soldiers, with inscriptions indicating that soldiers from the Sixth and Twentieth legions were both based here at some different times. This was when the existing civilian settlement developed into the town which can be seen today. According to Roman writers, sometime around the AD 180s, Hadrian's Wall was probably breached by northern invaders, which coincides with evidence of burning and destruction of buildings at Corbridge, showing that although the town was prosperous and guarded by the military, it could still have been prone to barbarian attacks.

To the south of the Roman town is the bridge that carried Dere Street over the River Tyne, and was a major crossing, carrying the main route into Scotland since the first century. There were several bridges on the site, with the latter one being the most ornate, indicating the prosperity of the town. Designed to impress, it had up to eleven stone arches and was 9 metres above the water level. It is unclear how long after the Roman period the bridge was in use, but at some point the stone was robbed, with some of it being reused in the building of the predecessor to Hexham Abbey. The River Tyne has continually changed course, and in 2004, part of the remains of the southern approach to the bridge were excavated because of the threat of erosion to the southern bank. The massive stones were moved from the river and can now be seen on the southern side of the river. The size of these stones shows how substantial the bridge would have been.

The museum at Corbridge is the best place to begin a site tour as it contains artefacts and inscriptions, all recovered from the town. Highlights include the Corbridge lion, one of five statues recovered from the site. It shows a lion pouncing on its prey (although no one knows if the prey is a sheep, cow, or goat). Archaeologists think the statue was originally part of a mausoleum or funerary monument, but at some point it was removed and repurposed as a water fountain in a grand house, with the water flowing from the lion's mouth. Another set of objects worth looking out for are part of the Corbridge hoard. Discovered in 1964, the hoard was a collection of objects including armour, leather, textiles, weapons and writing tablets, with the objects dating to sometime between AD 122 and 138. They were stored in a leather-covered wooden box, which was buried by the owner who expected to collect it at a later date, but never came back for it. As well as objects from the everyday lives of the residents of the town, it is worth looking out for one of the more mysterious objects in the collection: the dodecahedron. A copper 'ball' with twelve pentagonal faces and small knobs on the corners, around 100 of these unusual objects have been found, with this being the most northerly example. Archaeologists cannot decide what it was used for.

There are numerous interpretation signs around the site, but there are a few highlights to note. Running through the centre of the town is Dere Street, with the river bridge over the River Tyne to the south. Instead of running directly north towards Scotland, the line of the road was adjusted, so that visitors had to pass through the town. On the north side of Dere Street, and in front of the museum, are two granaries next to each other. Granaries are found in every Roman fort, with grain stored on a wooden floor, which was raised off the ground so that air could circulate through the building (the air vents can still be seen at ground level). This would also have protected the grain from vermin. Granaries have a unique shape and are easily identified by archaeologists because of the stone buttresses that stick out of the building, which would have supported the raised floor joists. To the right of the granaries are the remains of a stone trough. Originally, this was part of an elaborate fountain, forming the main water supply for the town. Few such examples of such an elaborate structure have been found it Britain and show how wealthy the settlement was. Next to this are the remains of a large courtyard building – note the large blocks of masonry that were used to construct the building. The size and ornateness of the few remaining building blocks have led archaeologists to speculate that it was an Imperial government building, possibly a forum or marketplace for the town, or may have been planned a headquarters building for a legionary fortress (a regional military base) which was never built. Within the main area of this building the outline of the earlier fort buildings can be seen.

Notice the strange sort of undulations in the ground, which are most prominent on the southern side of Dere Street. These have been caused by the subsidence of buildings being built on top of the foundations of earlier structures. Underneath this area, archaeologists uncovered the remains of several compounds, with an inscription found in one dating it to the second century. The purpose of these compounds is unknown, although one could have been used for industrial activity, indicated by some weapons and iron slag found during excavations, while the other may have been the site of additional accommodation for soldiers.

Directions & Accessibility: Corbridge Roman town is located to the north-west of the modern town and is well signposted from the A69. It has a small museum and toilets,

Granaries, Corbridge Roman town.

both of which are accessible (and dogs are allowed inside). There is no café, but there are
picnic benches by the museum. For those with limited mobility, it is possible to overlook the
remains from the museum, but the surface of the site itself is uneven and hazardous.

As well as visiting the Roman site, it is also worth exploring the modern town, where
there are excellent pubs, cafés and shops. Of particular note is Forum Books in the Old
Chapel, and Grants Bakery, both on the Market Place. There is some parking available in
the town, as well as a large public car park just over the river – this is the car park to use
if you want to visit the remains of the bridge. To visit the collection of stones that were
rescued from the river, follow the path that can be accessed from the north side of the car
park. The path is fairly level, and the stones are just under a kilometre along the river.

Hexham
Toilets | Parking
NY 934 640 | NE46 3NB | masterpiece.rebounder.startles

An old market town, Hexham, is the main settlement in this part of Northumberland, and
one to visit if a rest is needed from all things Roman. Many have suggested that there must
be a Roman fort underneath Hexham, and many of the towns in this part of England
have Roman origins, but there's no evidence for this at Hexham. But deep below Hexham
Abbey, there are some Roman remains. Or rather, there are the remains of the Church of St
Andrew, with only the crypt surviving. Built in the 670s, the church and crypt used Roman
stone in the foundations of the building. It had been assumed by some archaeologists
that the stonework was originally taken from a nearby Roman fort, lost beneath modern
Hexham. Recent analysis indicates that the stonework is similar in size and design to those
found at the remains of the Roman bridges at Chesters and Corbridge, which shows that
the structures over the rivers were the source of stone for the church. Hexham is a delightful

Hexham Abbey.

town to stay in and visit if you're exploring this part of Hadrian's Wall country with hotels, restaurants and a great selection of cafés. There are a range of historical attractions in the local area, including Hexham Abbey and its crypt of Roman stones. There's also the Old Gaol Museum, the oldest, purpose-built prison in England.

* *

Many people visiting Hadrian's Wall will first encounter the monument as they turn onto the Military Road (B6318) at the roundabout with the A69, and is the best way to experience the Wall if you're heading to the central or western sections. If approaching from the Newcastle end, or heading up onto the Wall via the A68, continue west onto the B6318 (the Military Road). This is the first stretch of road that gives an impression of the impact of Hadrian's Wall on the Northumbrian landscape, and after a mile or so, the surviving earthworks are visible to the south of the road, while the northern defences of the Wall and the ditch can be seen. This is one section where the Wall itself lies underneath the modern road. After about another mile or so, after passing the woods on the south side of the road, the view opens out, and the ditch is much more visible, running parallel with the road. After the woods, the vallum and raised mound on its south side are prominent for several miles.

Just before reaching Turret 26B (Brunton) it is worth stopping at Heaven field battle site and the beautiful St Oswald's Church, reputedly the location of a battle between Oswald of Bernicia and Cadwallon ap Cadfan of Gwynedd, which took place around AD 634. Cadwallon, who had the bigger force, was ravaging Northumbria until Oswald's forces forced them into battle. Oswald's army defeated the Welsh and apparently pursued Cadwallon, killing him somewhere near the Roman fort at Epiacum.

Originally the site of a Saxon church, St Oswald's is home to a Roman altar stone, which can be seen inside. There is no electricity to the church, and services are held by gaslight, while the organ is powered by a manual pump operated by foot. Turret 25b (St Oswald's) sat to the south-west of the church. There is a small layby, with a wooden cross marking the battle site, on the north side of the B6318, where visitors can park when visiting the church (NY 936 694 | NE46 4EY | templates.removable.whistle).

Heading west and descending the hill that is Brunton Bank, you're about to pass a fifteen-metre-long section of Hadrian's Wall on the south side of the road. This section, known as Planetrees, was saved when an antiquarian, William Hutton, intervened when the landowner was robbing the stone of Wall, convincing him to save this section. The remains at Planetrees demonstrate the change in the construction of Hadrian's Wall, with the foundations of the Broad Wall, visible here, being around 10 Roman feet thick, with the Narrow Wall, at 8 Roman feet constructed on top. There is no car park nearby, making this a more difficult section to visit, and there may be livestock in the field surrounding the site.

**

Turret 26B (Brunton)
Turret | No Facilities | Limited Parking
NY 921 698 | NE46 4HH | discussed.juggled.readings

The remains of the Wall and turret at Brunton are impressive, and only a brief detour from the main road. The turret was excavated in the 1870s and is around 2.5 metres high, making it one of the best-preserved structures on this part of the Wall. The adjacent Wall is an example of the Broad Wall and is around 2.6 metres high in places. To the north of the Wall is a section of ditch, and the berm can also be seen in front of the turret.

Directions & Accessibility: The nearest parking to the turret is in a small layby on the west side of the A6079. If heading on the B6318 towards Chesters Roman fort, take the left (signposted Hexham) at the crossroads with the A6079. The Wall and turret are signposted and visible from the main road and can be accessed by crossing the style. There are usually livestock here and dogs are not allowed in the field. Alternative parking is available at Chesters Roman fort (about thirty minutes' walk), following the Hadrian's Wall Path to the turret. The path is grassy in most places, and the turret on a steep hill.

Brunton turret.

Chesters Bridge
Bridge | No Facilities | No Parking
www.english-heritage.org.uk
NY 914 700 | NE46 4ES | during.flicks.blown

Across the river from the fort at Chesters are the substantial remains of one of the most important and impressive river crossings on Hadrian's Wall. Chesters Bridge is a hidden gem that is often missed by tourists to the Wall because it's off the beaten track and not too easy to get to.

The first crossing across the River North Tyne was a simple footbridge, designed to be practical and functional. At some point the bridge seems to have been replaced with one which could accommodate traffic, and which was around 58 metres long, with the road surface being 10 metres above the river. As Hadrian's Wall approaches the river, it ends at a guard tower, which marks the beginning of the bridge. The bridge abutment, which is visible today, further on from the tower, was originally in the river, but over the past 1,900 years, the course of the waterway has moved 15 metres to the west, leaving this section on dry land. The site was initially examined in the 1860s and again in the 1980s and 1990s, with archaeologists finding an inscription that suggests that there was a shrine to the nymphs of the river on or close to the bridge. When the river is particularly low, the west abutment of the second bridge, along with two piers, can be seen in the water. See the previous section on Hexham for the eventual destination of some of the robbed bridge stonework.

Directions & Accessibility: The entrance to the path that leads to the bridge is accessible from the south side of the more recent Chollerford Bridge, just before the traffic lights (NY 920 704 | NE46 4EN | washed.starfish.canine), with the site about a kilometre along the path. There is no parking nearby, and it may be easier for visitors to either park at the Brunton Turret layby (see the previous entry) or to park at Chesters fort and walk to the bridge (around thirty minutes).

Chesters bridge.

Hadrian's Wall: Centre

The natural boundary of the River North Tyne signifies the end of the eastern section and the beginning of the central section of Hadrian's Wall. Arguably, this is the most picturesque and intense as the Wall snakes over craggy outcrops and clings to the edge of cliffs. It also shows the remote, hostile and inhospitable landscape that the soldiers, stationed here 1,900 years ago, would have faced. This is Hadrian's Wall at its most dramatic.

Chesters
Cilurnum (Cauldron pool)
Fort | Bathhouse | Museum | Café | Toilets | Parking | Charge
www.english-heritage.org.uk
NY 910 704 | NE46 4EU | warblers.spending.quilt

The fort at Chesters can often be overlooked in favour of some of the more dramatic sites on Hadrian's Wall, but that's no reason not to visit this site. Chesters has a lot to offer: the best-preserved bathhouse on Hadrian's Wall, the nearby bridge remains (see the previous entry), a museum packed full of Roman objects, a great café, as well as the fort itself. If you're only able to visit a handful of sites, or just focussing on the sites in the central section of Hadrian's Wall, then Chesters is both a must-see site, and the perfect place to begin your tour.

Guarding the crossing over the River North Tyne, the fort was originally home to a cavalry unit of 500 men, who had their origins in Roman Spain and occupied the site for over 200 years. The fort was initially excavated in 1843 by the notable antiquarian John

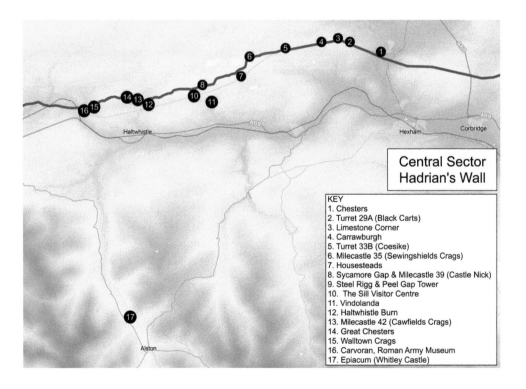

Central Sector Hadrian's Wall

KEY
1. Chesters
2. Turret 29A (Black Carts)
3. Limestone Corner
4. Carrawburgh
5. Turret 33B (Coesike)
6. Milecastle 35 (Sewingshields Crags)
7. Housesteads
8. Sycamore Gap & Milecastle 39 (Castle Nick)
9. Steel Rigg & Peel Gap Tower
10. The Sill Visitor Centre
11. Vindolanda
12. Haltwhistle Burn
13. Milecastle 42 (Cawfields Crags)
14. Great Chesters
15. Walltown Crags
16. Carvoran, Roman Army Museum
17. Epiacum (Whitley Castle)

Clayton, with sporadic excavations at the site during the first half of the twentieth century, and geophysical surveys in the latter part. The early excavations uncovered evidence of the Wall being bonded with the gatehouses on the east and west side of the fort. However, the course of the *vallum* remains a mystery – does it run to the south of the fort as happens at other fort sites on the Wall, or does it join the defensive ditches of the fort? During the excavation of the south gate, painted wall plaster was found in one of the guard chambers, along with a diploma dating to AD 146. This was an important document that was cast in bronze and awarded to soldiers who had served in the military for twenty-five years, giving them an honourable discharge and certain rights as veterans of the Roman army. Unfortunately, the original is in the British Museum, although a copy can be seen in the on-site museum. Like most forts on Hadrian's Wall, there was also a settlement surrounding Chesters, which may have covered as much as 15 hectares, making it one of the largest civilian sites on the Wall. The fort itself appears to have been abandoned in the fifth century.

The Clayton Museum (opposite the shop) is the perfect place to begin exploring the site. Named after John Clayton, the nineteenth-century antiquarian who did much to preserve Hadrian's Wall and its forts, and who also lived in a grand house on the edge of Chesters. The museum houses Clayton's personal collection of Roman objects and artefacts. Although many of the objects were found at Chesters, Clayton owned five forts along the Wall, and excavated many sites, with a lot of artefacts coming from elsewhere on the Wall.

As you enter the museum, don't forget to pay homage to gods at the digital altar, where you can find out about religion on the northern frontier. Established in the 1890s, stepping into the museum is very much like stepping into a bygone era, with the museum looking very similar to how it would have looked 130 years ago when it first opened. Despite the museum being quite small, there's are a huge number objects on display, including an impressive collection of stone altars and religious artefacts against one wall. At the back of the display is the elaborately carved stone arch that was discovered at Housesteads in the 1880s and belonged to the shrine of Mars Thincsus, the original location of which is unknown. The arch depicts the god Mars with a goose at his feet. The contents of Coventina's Well are also on display in the museum (see the entry for Carrawburgh Roman fort).

After exploring the museum, head back out and down the long path towards the fort. On your way there, look out for the 'binoculars', which you can look through to help visualise the site. Not all the fort has been excavated, and what can be seen are the buildings uncovered during the nineteenth-century excavations. At the end of the path are the remains of the north gate of the fort and are a standard design found at forts across the Wall. The gatehouse had two towers, on each side of the gate entrances or portals, within which were guard chambers. In the distance, on the right are the exposed remains of the western gatehouse, while the big house behind it was once occupied by John Clayton. To the south are another set of exposed buildings, this time barrack blocks, which would also have housed horses in each of the rooms.

Passing between the barrack block and another set of buildings takes visitors through the east gate and towards the river and the bathhouse. On the left, after passing out of the fort, is another section of Hadrian's Wall which would have originally joined the bridge across the River North Tyne. There's now a viewing platform overlooking the river, almost on the exact line of the bridge. There are a few stones from the bridge in the river, while across on the other bank are the remains of the buttress of the bridge that crossed the river and is accessible to visitors. The river has moved course since the Roman period, leaving the remains high and dry (see the previous entry).

The bathhouse at Chesters is one of the best-preserved examples of such a building in Britain. Heading down the steps into the site and entering the building takes visitors into the original changing rooms, with the niches against the back wall possibly being used to store clothes. The next room along is a lobby leading into a warm room, then into the steam room. The apse on the east side of this room probably had a fountain in it, with a hot room beyond this. On left of the lobby is the cold plunge pool room, with a warm room beyond this. At the end of that room is a small arch where warm air was pushed through from a furnace, heating the space under the floor. The remains of the *hypocaust* floor (raised floors on little pillars with air between them to circulate the hot air) can still be seen here and in the commanding officer's house. During excavation of the bathhouse, the skeletons of two dogs and a horse were found, along with a more macabre discovery – thirty-three human skeletons. It is unclear how they died or how they ended up in a mass grave at the bathhouse.

Returning to the fort, towards the centre is the headquarters building, and on the left, closest to the gate, are the baths for the commanding officer's house and the building itself. Some archaeologists believe that this bathhouse was used by all the soldiers occupying the fort and not just the commanding officer. The baths have a good example of a *hypocaust* floor, with some pillars supporting the floor being made of tiles salvaged from some other part of the fort.

Entering the headquarters building through the main entrance takes visitors into a courtyard, with a series of rooms at the rear. Don't forget to look for the *phallus* carved into a flagstone on the north side – it is big enough to be a trip hazard! Within the centre

Bathhouse, Chesters fort.

of the rooms at the back of the buildings is the treasury vault, an underground space where money and booty were stored. When the headquarters was excavated in the 1830s, the original metal studded door to the treasury survived, but crumbled soon after it was found.

Directions & Accessibility: Chesters fort, near the village of Chollerford, is signposted from the main routes. There are no formal paths on site, and the ground is grassy with some bumps, although flat (except at the bathhouse where access is via steps). Those with some mobility issues will probably find this one of the more accessible sites on the Wall to visit, although it is still advisable to contact English Heritage or check their website.

* *

From Chesters fort, head west along the B6318. Almost immediately on the right are the impressive and grand stables for Walwick Hall. Originally constructed in 1891, they have recently been converted into holiday accommodation. Continuing west, the road climbs the hill past Walwick Hall and as the tress clear towards the summit, there's a view of another preserved section of the Wall, while on the north side, the remains of the ditch and berm can be seen. The vallum, which should be on the south side of the road, isn't yet visible.

After the crossroads and the small wooded area, the ditch is again visible on the north side of the road. This is also the location of Milecastle 29 (Tower Tyre), although the only remains are depressions in the ground. A little further on, and visible in the distance on the north side of the road, are two stretches of the Wall, along with Turret 29A (Black Carts).

* *

Turret 29A (Black Carts)
Turret | No Facilities | Limited Parking
NY 884 712 | NE46 4BL | agency.doctors.removals

One of the more impressive surviving sections of Hadrian's Wall, along with a turret, Black Carts heralds the beginning of a long stretch where there are visible remains of the forward and rear defences. The Wall and turret have been excavated on a number of occasions, with coins from different periods discovered. The most recent excavations took place in the 1990s, with archaeologists discovering that the ditch on the north side of Wall was only 3.5 metres wide and 2.8 metres wide, which is much less than the dimensions at other sections of the Wall. The archaeologists also found evidence of ploughing, and even hoofprints beneath the bank which form part of the Wall defences. Analysis of pollen recovered during the excavations indicates that when the Wall was being built, the area was open grassland rather than woodland. The *vallum* was also explored and was found to be 6 metres wide and 2.8 metres deep, with the bottom 1.3 metres cut through rock. There was also some sign of a road surface, like a track on the north berm of the *vallum*.

Directions & Accessibility: The site at Black Carts is divided by the minor road, with the turret being on the downhill (eastern) side, and a longer stretch of Wall and ditch further uphill. To reach the site, visitors can park on the minor road where there is space for a single vehicle, or carry on along the road where there is a small layby about half a kilometre on the left, although the road is quite narrow and there are no turning spaces for quite a distance.

There are no paths around the site, with the area being grassed. The eastern part of the site is accessible through a gate, while the other section can be reached by climbing through a gap in the wall.

Hadrian's Wall, Black Carts.

**

Head back onto the B6318 and go west. On the north side of the road is a particularly long section of Wall (or you can walk the couple of kilometres alongside the Wall from Black Carts to Limestone Corner). In this section of Wall are the remains of Turret 29b (Limestone Bank).

**

Limestone Corner
Ditch | No Facilities | Limited Parking
NY 874 715 | NE46 4DB | trickster.slurping.unicorns

Without a doubt, Limestone Corner is one of the more unusual sections of Hadrian's Wall. On the south side of the road runs the *vallum*, although it is partly overgrown due to the plantation. The *vallum* is cut through a distinct section of quartz dolerite (the name Limestone Corner is rather misleading) and demonstrates how impressive Roman engineering was.

On the north side of the road, the ditch also cuts through quartz dolerite, but construction or quarrying of the ditch was never completed, and most of the stone has not been removed, with several large pieces lying on the berms and in the ditch, awaiting removal. Presumably, the Romans decided it was too much effort to move the blocks if they were not needed elsewhere.

Directions & Accessibility: Heading west on the B6318, Black Carts, Limestone Corner is on the bend in the road. Immediately after this, on the north side of the road, is a small layby beside a field gate. There is a gap in the wall to enter the field, with the quarried ditch in front. The vallum is in the plantation and fields on the south side of the road. Given the stone remains, the access may be difficult for those with mobility issues.

Ditch, Limestone Corner.

Carrawburgh
Brocolitia (badgers)
Fort | Temple | No Facilities | Parking
www.english-heritage.org.uk
NY 860 712 | NE46 4DB | counters.major.reckoned

Carrawburgh fort lacks the impressiveness of many other forts on and around Hadrian's Wall, but is one of the few sites where the remains of a temple can be seen. Carrawburgh is also where Coventina's Well, a Roman shrine, was excavated in the nineteenth century, and contained many Roman artefacts that were deliberately hidden.

There are no significant remains to be seen at Carrawburgh fort, it is possible to make out the ramparts, and on the south side two of the defensive ditches, although it probably had a third ditch, which has been erased through ploughing. The site becomes overgrown with vegetation in the summer, but when the grass is low, it is possible to see the earthworks of some of the internal buildings. The main east and west entrances to the fort are visible as gaps in the ramparts. The north gate, rampart and ditches lie under the modern road.

This is an important site because archaeologists have demonstrated that it overlies the *vallum*, which indicates that it was not part of the original plan for the Wall. However, excavation on the defences has revealed that the corner towers of the fort, on the north side, were set into the curtain wall. This helps to show that the original plan for the Wall did not involve constructing forts, but after digging the *vallum*, the plan changed and these were added in. Excavations at Carrawburgh have been limited, but these investigations have shown that fort had a similar internal design to other fort on the Wall, while work in 1873, undertaken by John Clayton, uncovered the bathhouse to the south-west of the fort, which had the standard layout for such buildings on Hadrian's Wall.

Carrawburgh has the most complete remains of a Mithraic temple on the Wall. Such temples are usually subterranean or partly submerged to represent the cave at the heart of the cults foundation myth, and the site at Carrawburgh was excavated around the 1950s, with archaeologists concluding that several buildings had occupied the site over the years. The earliest temple they found dated to the early third century and existed for about a hundred years. It was subsequently extended and reconfigured over the next century, but was abandoned after this. The roof was removed and the statues damaged, with some archaeologists suspecting the damage may have been done by Christians rising up against the cult. There are replicas of three altars in the ruins of the Mithraeum, which would have originally been painted bright colours. One of these, dedicated to the sun god Sol, would have had a candle placed in the recess, lighting up rays of sun carved into the stone. The original altar stones can be seen in the Great North Museum in Newcastle, where there is also a replica of the Mithraeum.

North-west of the Mithraeum is the site of Coventina's Well, a shrine dedicated to a water goddess. Excavated in the nineteenth century, a huge number of objects, including coins and small statues, all of which were probably offerings, were recovered from the well. Archaeologists have speculated that the objects may have been dumped in the well and covered over with debris, with stones from the shrine removed and placed on top of the well to hide it. Many of the items discovered in Coventina's Well are on display in the museum at Chesters Roman Fort.

Directions & Accessibility: Car parking is plentiful here, although it is pay and display. There are no visible features in the fort, except for the defences. Although the fort is not particularly notable, the Mithraeum is worth visiting. Follow the track around the fort defences, staying outside the fence. On the west side, the ground slopes down towards the Mithraeum, a fenced in area which is often liable to flooding. Coventina's Well is northwest of the Mithraeum. However, the land is particularly boggy all year round, with reeds hiding the well site, so approaching it is not recommended.

There is no formal path at Carrawburgh, and access for those with mobility issues will be challenging as the route around the site can often be muddy and slippy, particularly when approaching the Mithraeum. Livestock is usually in the field for most of the year, so caution is urged, particularly with dogs.

Mithraeum, Carrawburgh.

* *

From Carrawburgh continue west along the main road, which runs on top of the Wall foundations. On the north side, the ditch is still visible, while to the south, the vallum runs alongside the road, although it is only visible intermittently. After a couple of miles, the road moves slightly to the left towards a slight summit where the mounds and vallum are particularly visible and close to the road, as is the ditch on the north side.

As you approach the small lake, Shield-on-the-Wall dam, on the north side of the road are the remains of Milecastle 33 (Shield-on-the-Wall), visible as a small mound covered in the vegetation. Continue further on, past the ruined farm building, to where the road turns slightly to the left into a wooded area. At this point, Hadrian's Wall separates from the beneath the B6318 and continues on a parallel course, with Turret 33B (Coesike) about 40 metres along the Wall from this point.

* *

Turret 33B (Coesike)
Turret | No Facilities | No Parking
NY 830 707 | NE47 7AL | pushes.chromatic.scarves

Coesike Turret is part of a small section of the Wall, which survives to around four courses. Excavations at the site found pig, sheep and cattle bones, which may have been the remnants of animals butchered by the soldiers.

Directions & Accessibility: Coesike is set back from the main road, and difficult to reach from the main road as there are no laybys or lanes to park in. The best way to see the turret is to park at Housesteads and walk to the site, along the Hadrian's Wall Path, around a 5 km walk with steep and craggy sections. The path will not be suitable for those with mobility issues.

Milecastle 35 (Sewingshields Crags)
Viewpoint | Milecastle | No Facilities | Parking
NY 800 700 | NE47 7AL | firebird.stripped.plants

Sewingshields Crags is one of the most dramatic sections of Hadrian's Wall, but must also have been an engineering challenge for the Romans given that it snakes its way across the landscape, up and down the Crags until it reaches the western sector. Seeing the Wall in the driving wind and snow of autumn shows what an inhospitable environment this must have been 1,900 years ago, and you cannot but pity the soldiers from warmer climes who were posted here.

The Milecastle was excavated at the end of the 1970s, with a section of Broad Wall visible on the northern side. Unusually, the excavators didn't find evidence of a gate on the north side of the milecastle, which would have enabled and also controlled people moving through the Wall, although some archaeologists argue this must have existed.

Directions & Accessibility: Sewingshields Crags is not readily accessible from the main road. The best way to visit the site is to approach it from Housesteads fort where you can park (pay and display). Follow the path, accessed from the car park, up towards the fort (there's no need to access the English Heritage site), and follow the Hadrian's Wall Path east. The views on the way to the Crags, as well as on top of them, make the trip worthwhile.

Hadrian's Wall and Sewingshields Crags.

The wall that runs towards the Crags is, mostly, a more recent field boundary, and it is not until you reach them that you get glimpses of Hadrian's Wall, albeit only the foundations. From the top, you get excellent views to the north and south, and it isn't difficult to see why the Romans built the Wall in this location. There are no substantial remains of Turret 35a (Sewingshields Crags), which is near the summit, but it is worth continuing a short distance east to the Milecastle and a large stretch of Wall foundations.

Housesteads
Vercovicium (hilly place or place of the fighters)
Fort | Museum | Café | Toilets | Parking | Charge
www.english-heritage.org.uk
NY 793 684 | NE47 6NN | tungsten.token.outings

The remains of Housesteads fort are arguably the most impressive of the Roman forts on Hadrian's Wall. Its dramatic positioning on a rocky outcrop effectively displays the abilities of the Roman engineers. The fort would have been an intimidating and impressive site to those approaching it, although on a wet or snowy day, the settlement outside must have been a bleak place to live. Even today, the wind and rain at Housesteads can be unforgiving, but if you had to choose a single site to visit, then this is it.

Housesteads has been investigated by antiquarians and archaeologists many times over the centuries. The first excavations, which took place in the 1830s, were among the earliest to take place on Hadrian's Wall, with more extensive work taking place in the late nineteenth century, and again a century later. The fort itself is remarkably well preserved, with many of the internal buildings uncovered for visitors to explore, while the defensive walls of the fort stand eleven courses high in places. An account from the early nineteenth century states the fort was surrounded by three ditches and ramparts, although only one can be seen today. The ditches on the south side of the fort appear to have been removed early in the third century to enable the civilian settlement to expand.

There is also evidence for a temple of Mithras to the southeast of the fort. Other temples have been located at Carrawburgh and Rudchester forts. Discovered in 1822 and excavated at the end of that century, a carving from the temple, which is now in the onsite museum, has the earliest depiction of the zodiac in Britain. The carving shows Mithras emerging from an egg, while surrounding him are the signs of the zodiac. Several altars were also recovered from the site, although these are now in the Great North Museum in Newcastle. The temple site is now a stony depression and there are no significant remains to be seen.

Before ascending to the fort, which is a steep climb in places, look out for the blackboard at the entrance where the latest wildlife and birds of prey seen at the site are recorded. Towards the top of the hill, the path forks right to the fort, or left to the small museum. Visiting the museum is a good opportunity to get your breath back. The museum is a replica of a Roman building from the settlement outside the fort and has many of the finds from the site on display. One worth looking for is a carved slab that features three hooded figures, known as the *genii cuculatti* (hooded spirits), which are representations of local deities. Another item is the metal flask, which belonged to a soldier and was discovered in one of the barrack blocks.

Heading towards the fort, the remains of the civilian settlement can be seen in front of the fort and on either side of the path. The settlement comprised wooden buildings were built on turf foundations, although there were also some buildings built from stone. Around twenty-seven buildings were excavated in the 1930s, although there are still more to be explored. One in particular, the most easterly building (which is signposted), hid a grizzly secret. Now known as the Murder House, during the excavations, two skeletons were discovered underneath the floor. The first skeleton, a middle-aged man, had been stabbed, with the end of a dagger still sticking out of his ribs. The cause of death of the second skeleton was unclear, but it seems likely that they too were also murdered. The murders appear to have taken place in the fourth century, but before the settlement was abandoned around AD 367.

On entering the fort, the first building on the right is a bastle house, known as Bardon Mill, which was built in the sixteenth or seventeenth century in the ruins of the east guard tower of the gatehouse. These fortified houses were built to secure the occupants against raiders from Scotland known as Border reivers.

The fort itself is easy to get around, although the north-west and south-west quadrants remain unexcavated. Highlights worth exploring include the central range of buildings, which begin on the left of the entrance and follow the path up the hill. The first building is the commander's house, with the headquarters building next, and the hospital to the left of it. At the top of the hill are the granaries. Beyond the granaries is the northern defensive wall of the fort, which doubled up as Hadrian's Wall, and can be seen as it snakes over the crags to the east. By the northern gate are several sunken pits, which were used to gather water as there are no natural springs at Housesteads. To the east there is an excavated barrack block.

In the middle of the eastern wall of the fort are the remains of the gatehouse, beyond which the remains of the bathhouse were discovered in the nineteenth century along with evidence of industrial workings. To the east of the fort, there is a hollow or depression in the ground, which some archaeologists believe may have been a Roman amphitheatre, a space where people would have been entertained by various blood sport and fights. The site has never been excavated, but it seems an unlikely location for such a building.

Continuing along the inside walls of the fort and down the slope is an impressive and unusual site – an original Roman toilet block that is so well preserved. The only thing that is missing are the actual toilet seats, which would have been made of stone or wood with a hole in it and

Granaries, Housesteads.

would have been particularly cold to sit on, especially in the winter! There's an original wooden toilet seat on display at Vindolanda fort. The toilets would also have been communal and you would have sat with your friends as you used the facilities. Quite a different experience today.

Directions & Accessibility: Housesteads Roman fort is signposted on all the major routes in the area. There is plenty of parking (pay and display) at the site, with toilets by the entrance and at the museum up by the fort. The café is located in the building by the car park at the site entrance, although some refreshments can be bought in the museum.

The path to the fort is stony, uneven and very steep in places. There is often livestock in the fields surrounding the fort, although dogs on a lead are welcome. Some arrangements can be made directly with English Heritage for those with limited mobility to be taken to the museum, but even from that point, there is quite a climb within the fort where there are steps, with no formal paths beyond the entrance. Housesteads is very close to The Sill, Steel Rigg and Vindolanda fort. Combining a trip to Housesteads with Vindolanda will take the best part of a day, and is recommended if you can only visit two sites on Hadrian's Wall.

Sycamore Gap & Milecastle 39 (Castle Nick)
Viewpoint | Milecastle | No Facilities | No Parking
nationaltrust.org.uk
NY 761 677 | NE47 7AW | warmers.vesting.index

One of the most photographed sections of Hadrian's Wall, Sycamore Gap is where the Wall makes its way over Highshield Crags, dropping and then climbing its way up Peel Crags. There are two sites to see here. The first, when approaching from the east, is Sycamore Gap, a scenic viewpoint that was featured in the film *Robin Hood: Prince of Thieves*. The Gap is where a solitary sycamore tree sits in a low point between two hills. From here, the Wall continues west to another dip where the remains of Milecastle 39 (Castle Nick) can be seen.

Sycamore Gap.

The milecastle has been excavated on three occasions, and the remains stand to about eight courses high in places, and the stone foundations of internal buildings can be seen.

Directions & Accessibility: Sycamore Gap and Castle Nick are two sites that are challenging to reach by car, as there are no laybys on the B6318. It is better to park at The Sill or Steel Rigg (see below) and walk along the Wall from the latter site. There is a particularly steep climb to the top of the Crags.

Steel Rigg & Peel Gap Tower
Viewpoint | Tower | Parking
northumberlandnationalpark.org.uk
NY 712 665 | NE49 9PJ | kingpin.searching.slope

Steel Rigg, the collective name for the area that covers Peel Crags, Sycamore Gap and Highshield Crags, is one of the more dramatic sections of Hadrian's Wall. Even though climbing to the top of the Crags is challenging, it is worth it for the tremendous views of the Northumbrian countryside.

From the car park, follow the path which takes you past Hadrian's Wall and down towards the remains of Peel Gap tower. The tower was only discovered in 1987 and was positioned here to fill a weak point in the defences of the Wall, plugging a gap between two turrets. From here make the challenging and steep ascent up onto Steel Rigg using the steps cut into the rock. At the top of the Crags, Hadrian's Wall crosses the summit, close to the cliff edge, and stands to a height of nine courses in places. On the summit is Turret 39a where the bodies of a young man and woman were discovered during excavation. It is not clear how they died or when they were buried, but it seems to have been before the tower underwent modifications in the late second century.

Directions & Accessibility: From the B6318, take a right at the crossroads (signposted) where The Sill Visitor Centre is located and head north up the minor road. At the top of the

Steel Rigg, Hadrian's Wall.

hill is the car park (pay and display) for Steel Rigg. It is a small car park and the adjacent field is used as an overflow. There is often livestock in the fields surrounding the car park. Visitors should note that the steps down to Peel Gap tower, and the subsequent climb up onto Steel Rigg, is both steep and hazardous, but worthwhile.

The Sill: National Landscape Discovery Centre
Visitor Centre | Café | Toilets | Parking
www.thesill.org.uk
NY 752 668 | NE47 7AN | mistress.momentous.alien

A relative newcomer to Hadrian's Wall, The Sill opened in 2017 and is billed as the gateway to the Northumberland National Park. It functions as a as an exhibition space, education centre and promotes the UNESCO World Heritage Site status of Hadrian's Wall. The Sill has a permanent exhibition focussing on the landscape, culture and heritage of the National Park, as well as temporary exhibitions on various topics such as the geology of the Wall. There's also a tourist information centre, a shop selling local produce, and a large café.

Through The Sill, the National Park has an extensive education programme, with regular family-focussed events, and teachers can even borrow boxes of archaeological artefacts, helping to explore history in the classroom. There is also a modern youth hostel attached to The Sill, providing a perfect base from which to explore the central section of Hadrian's Wall, with the impressive section of the Wall at Steel Rigg, along with Peel Gap tower only a fifteen-minute walk to the north, while Vindolanda is ten minutes away by car.

Directions & Accessibility: The Sill is located on the B6318 at Twice Brewed and is signposted from the major routes in the area. While The Sill is free to enter, there is a charge for the car park. The site is fully accessible.

Vindolanda (Chesterholm)

Vindolanda (white enclosure or white lawn)
Fort | Museum | Café | Toilets | Parking | Charge
www.vindolanda.com
NY 767 663 | NE47 7JP | trump.listed.curly

Better known by its Latin name, Vindolanda, the fort here is one of the most notable and well-known Roman sites in the world, and is a must-see for anyone visiting Hadrian's Wall. The site has been extensively excavated over the centuries, and there continues to be an ongoing long-term programme of archaeological exploration, with visitors able to tour the areas being excavated every year. It's a fascinating site with new discoveries being made every day, and along with nearby Housesteads fort, it is one that everyone should definitely see when they make the trip to Hadrian's Wall.

Vindolanda is one of the first sites where Romans remains were recorded in the modern era, with an account appearing in a sixteenth-century book, but it wasn't until 1716 that the site was first dug. More excavations took place in the early nineteenth century, with subsequent pockets of digging taking place throughout the rest of the century. It's not until towards the middle of the twentieth century that the programme of excavation gave us the site we see today. Our knowledge of the site is constantly changing as it gives up its secrets, and there have been many exciting and important finds from Vindolanda, with the most well known being a large stash of writing tablets. These fragments of writing tablets and *papyri* (reed paper) were found at the site, some in the remains of a bonfire outside the fort. The tablets offer an insight into aspects of life at Vindolanda that aren't normally visible during archaeological investigations, such as invitations to a birthday party and requests for clothing. Modern excavations have been going on for over fifty years, and along with more recent geophysical surveys of the site and surrounding area, there is a substantial amount of knowledge about both military and civilian life at Vindolanda. There are at least nine forts, all built on top of each other with some being bigger than others, with the earliest ones built with timber buildings and defences on turf foundations. These lie some 4 metres underneath the current ground level. Later forts were built out of stone and are visible at the site today.

Originally constructed as a fort on the Stanegate in the first century, Vindolanda continued to be occupied once Hadrian's Wall was constructed and operational, with soldiers garrisoning the Wall being based at the fort. Even after the Hadrian's Wall was abandoned in favour of the Antonine Wall, the fort continued in use and may have been converted to stone around this time. The fort remained in use until the latter half of the fourth century, and may have continued to have been occupied in the earliest part of the fifth century, although the surrounding settlement only lasted until the late third century. The reasons for its abandonment are unclear.

Vindolanda is a large site, and there is a lot to do and see here, so it is worth putting aside at least half a day for a visit, if not longer. The visitor centre at the site entrance has both a film presentation introducing the site and a model of the site. From the visitor centre, the path passes by the remains of the civil settlement in front of the western gate of the fort. The visible remains primarily date to the third and four centuries, and include workshops and a temple to an unknown indigenous deity. There is also some evidence that there may have been a market in this area at some point. The main path leads to the south, or visitors can join the original Roman road into the fort. Inside the fort, it is possible to see the remains of the central range of buildings, with the granaries being on the west side, followed by the headquarters building, and then the commander's house.

After exploring the central range, visit the north side of the fort where the cavalry barracks are preserved. Before exploring beyond the north gate, notice the semi-circular stone foundations that are dotted around the site, and which some archaeologists have compared to the footprint of Iron Age roundhouses, although those are normally built from wood. These stone buildings have only been found at Vindolanda, and some archaeologists have suggested that they were built to house either locally conscripted soldiers who took part in the third-century Severan invasion of Scotland or were where prisoners of war were kept. Whatever these buildings were, and their real purpose, remains a bit of a mystery. Through the north gate result from recent excavations where the defences of some of the earlier forts, along with a section of road have been uncovered.

The southern quarter of the fort has been excavated recently, and the volunteer excavators have uncovered cavalry barracks from the later fort, and some possible evidence of a later church built within existing buildings in the fourth century. To the untrained eye, the excavated areas can look like a jumble of stones, but the excavation team are always happy to answer questions and point out what can be seen. A little way through the south gate are the remains of the bathhouse for the fort, which was built before the Hadrianic period at the site. The remains are well preserved and the pillars of the *hypocaust* heated floor system are still visible. The nearby recreated sections of Hadrian's Wall, one of turf and one of timber can be explored, and there are great views of the site from the tops of the towers.

Following the path to the east, takes visitors to a little glade, where a stream runs past some recreated and very colourful Roman buildings, showing how much more colourful life would have been in the Roman period. The buildings are normally to visitors and have various displays in them. On the right-hand side of the path, just before the museum is a replica Roman kiln, which is fired up during the summer months and you can see Roman pottery being made using the same methods as the Romans – details of when the kiln is being fired can be found online.

Vindolanda.

The museum has a wealth of Roman artefacts, most excavated from the site at Vindolanda, and there's also a small conservation laboratory where you can occasionally see work being undertaken to preserve some objects found on site. The museum contains many of the latest discoveries, some of them pulled out of the ground only days beforehand. Highlights to look out for include some of the original writing tablets on display in a special room, and the original leather boxing gloves, which may have had lead weights sown into them to do more damage to opponents! Or look out for some of the hundreds and hundreds of shoes discovered during the excavations. There's also the new gallery, which opened in 2018, and houses a collection of wooden objects recovered from the site, including a child's toy sword and an original Roman toilet seat!

The gift shop is probably the best of all the sites along Hadrian's Wall, with lots of unique and quirky gifts and a good selection of books focussing on the Romans and Hadrian's Wall. The café is also worth a visit, and again probably the best on the Wall. Vindolanda also has a regular programme of interesting events throughout the year (not just in the summer months), so it is worth checking out the website for details of what's on.

Directions & Accessibility: Vindolanda is signposted from all the major routes. As the excavations are part of an ongoing programme of work on the site, different areas can be closed off or may have restricted access, with the website giving details on what can be seen. There is an ongoing programme of events and activities for families, with site tours taking place every day, which are a great way to see learn about the history of the site and to find out what is currently being excavated. Excavations take place between April and September. The website is packed with information about both sites, and information on where to stay and eat in the local area.

Bathhouse, Vindolanda.

When visiting, it is best to start at the main entrance rather than from the eastern side where the museum is. For those with mobility issues, it is possible to park where the museum/café/gift shop are, especially as there is quite a steep hill between the fort and museum building. The site is very accessible, with excellent paths around the fort, although the interior of the fort is more uneven, and the museum building is fully accessible. It is possible to get a joint ticket for Vindolanda and The Roman Army Museum at Carvoran fort, a fifteen-minute drive away.

**

From Vindolanda or The Sill, head west on the B6318. Hadrian's Wall continues to follow the line of the various crags on the north side of the road. The vallum crosses under the road, and can be seen, a little way back, on the north side as you pass the Twice Brewed pub (next to The Sill).

**

Haltwhistle Burn
Fortlet | No Facilities | No Parking
NY 714 661 | NE49 9NN | obvious.inhales.highbrow

Located close to Hadrian's Wall, the small fort at Haltwhistle Burn was originally constructed on the Stanegate, and was one of the first sites to be formally surveyed in the early nineteenth century. The ramparts of the fort are constructed from turf, and the remains are still visible at the site, along with several other surviving earthworks. Excavated at the beginning of the twentieth century, the east gate had been replaced by a wall at some unknown time, while many of the internal buildings had stone foundations. Archaeologists have speculated that because of its size, the fortlet was probably occupied by a detachment from a garrison based elsewhere rather than being home to a cohort. Nearby, there are visible earthworks from several Roman camps, which probably houses soldiers building the fort as well as the Wall. The fortlet, and some of the surrounding camps, were geophysically surveyed in 2016. Not only were the earthworks visible, but there was also evidence for Roman ovens outside of some of the sites.

Directions & Accessibility: Heading west on the B6318, take the right to Cawfields, opposite the Milecastle Inn (signposted Cawfield Crags). The fortlet is just before the bend in the minor road, although there is no parking here, so continue to the Northumberland National Park-owned car park at Cawfields. From here, visitors can either follow the path which starts by the entrance to the car park at Cawfield Crags. Head south to the fortlet, or north if visiting Great Chesters fort. Alternatively, visit Milecastle 42 (see the next entry), which is a five-minute walk from the car park, and is alongside a spectacular stretch of Hadrian's Wall. From there take the path that crosses over the vallum and across the road to the fortlet site.

Milecastle 42 (Cawfields Crags)
Viewpoint | Milecastle | Toilets | Parking
northumberlandnationalpark.org.uk
NY 712 665 | NE49 9PJ | kingpin.searching.slope

Cawfields is another particularly scenic point on Hadrian's Wall, with dramatic views looking back east as the Wall clings to the edge of the craggy outcrops. It is also a good

Cawfields Crags milecastle.

point from which to explore the remains of Milecastle 42 (Cawfields Crags), as well as Turret 41A (Caw Gap), and even beyond, following the visible remains of the Wall for several kilometres.

Milecastle 42 was initially examined by John Clayton, who also excavated Chesters Roman Fort in 1848, and then again in the early part of the twentieth century. Like most milecastles, this one was an access point to get through the Wall. The entrance through the Wall can still be seen, as can the pivot hole which enabled the gate to turn.

Directions & Accessibility: From the B6318, follow the signs to Cawfield Crags (see the entry for Haltwhistle Burn above). There is a car park (pay and display) and toilets here. The car park has also been designated a Dark Sky Discovery Site, so is perfect for viewing the night sky. From the car park, follow the path around the north side of the quarry lake to the Wall with the milecastle is through the Wall on the left, while to the right, the small peak caused by quarrying can be climbed with excellent views of the surrounding area from the top. In the fields to the south of the Wall and milecastle are the visible remains of the vallum with the north and south mounds. Carry on the path past the milecastle, to the west for around 2 kilometres and you'll come to the remains of Turret 41a (Caw Gap). The paths in the area are grassed and can be muddy and steep in places.

Great Chesters
Aesica
Fort | No Access
NY 703 667 | NE49 9NE | drums.trades.bleaching

The fort at Great Chesters, which is probably named after an indigenous god, Esus or Hesus, is one of the better-preserved sites on Hadrian's Wall. It was also one of the last forts to be constructed as part of Hadrian's Wall. The site survives within a farm, with the surviving walls of the fort standing to an impressive height, around nine courses in places.

While there are some visible remains of the foundations of some of the internal buildings, including the barrack blocks, it really is the defensive wall, standing up to seven courses high in places, surrounding the fort that is the most impressive part of the site, although the arch, a surviving part of the ceiling of the sunken strong room, is not to be missed. The arch is within the fenced area at the centre of the fort. Recent analysis of the landscape around the fort has shown that there are a lot of hidden features, probably belonging to the civilian settlement, which are awaiting further exploration by archaeologists. There was also an aqueduct, which took water to the fort, but rather than being the ornate and fancy structures that people usually associate with aqueducts in the Roman period, this was a channel cut into the ground and covered over with stones. Just outside of the west side of the fort, it's possible to make out three of the ditches which originally surrounded the fort, but sadly now have been eroded away by ploughing.

Follow the line of the fort wall to the south. Halfway along are the remains of several buildings and the west gate, with guard houses on either side and some of the large stone foundations still in their original position. Continue to follow the wall, passing the south-west corner tower and eventually coming to the southern gate on the east side if the fort where an original Roman altar stands in the ruins of the gate guard tower. The altar has stood here for over a hundred years, but it probably came from somewhere in the settlement. On top of the altar, people have recently started leaving modern coins as offerings to the god that the altar was dedicated to. However, there doesn't appear to be an inscription on the stone, so whoever it's dedicated to will forever remain a mystery.

Directions & Accessibility: From the entrance to Cawfield Crags car park (see the previous entry), follow the path through the wall and up the hill towards the farm in the distance. There are several large styles to cross, and the fields can be wet and muddy and often contain livestock. The modern farm wall, running parallel with the path, is built on top of Hadrian's Wall, and if you peer over it, you can see the remains of the ditch, which still keeps much of its original dimensions. As you approach the farm, the path crosses a style

Great Chesters.

which is also the eastern wall of the fort. The path, which continues to be grassed and can be wet and muddy, takes you across the site, by the farm buildings (the farm being on top of the Wall).

Walltown Crags & Turret 45A (Walltown)
Wall |Viewpoint | Visitors Centre | Toilets | Parking
NY 668 659 | CA8 7HY | chill.gearing.lyricism

Some of the most spectacular views of Hadrian's Wall can be seen from Walltown Crags, which was itself a quarry that was closed and landscaped in the 1970s. From the top of the Crags are spectacular views to the north and south, while the Wall can be followed for almost 140 metres to the east, with the remains of Turret 45A (Walltown) also visible.

Directions & Accessibility: Follow the signs to the Roman Army Museum (signposted on all major routes), but carry on past the museum to Walltown Country Park (pay and display). Designated a Dark Sky Discovery Site, there are toilets and a small visitor centre with seasonal opening hours. To get to the Wall, follow the Pennine Way path, which is at the eastern end of the site. The path eventually leads up to Walltown Crags, from which there are spectacular views to the north and south, along with several turrets and milecastles to be seen, including the enigmatically named King Arthur's Well, a possible Roman site but associated with the mythical king who is said to lie asleep in a cave under the Crags.

Carvoran & the Roman Army Museum
Magna (stone or rock)
Fort | Museum | Café | Toilets | Parking | Charge
www.vindolanda.com/roman-army-museum
Fort: NY 667 656 | CA8 7HY | stammer.kitchens.lengthen
Museum: NY 666 657 | CA8 7H | squeezed.maternal.thickens

Carvoran is a Roman fort with little to be seen on the surface, but lots going on underneath. However, it is the nearby Roman Army Museum (and Walltown Crags) that makes a trip to this site worthwhile.

There has been little archaeological investigation of the site, with some brief work in the 1970s, and again at the turn of the twentieth century. However, this may change, with a programme of exploration and rescue archaeology being planned for the site, which has been affected by climate change and a drop in the water levels at the site. Geophysical surveying of the site has taken place and has shown many of the internal features of the fort, and that it was surrounded by a substantial civil settlement. Unusually, the *vallum* passes around the site to the north, while the Stanegate passes to the south. The fort also sits at the crossroads of the Stanegate and the Maiden Way, which heads south to the fort at Epiacum (Whitley Castle). The fort is privately owned, and it is not possible to visit, but it can be seen from the grounds of the Roman Army Museum.

There is enough to see and do in the museum to keep visitors, especially younger ones, occupied for several hours. There are galleries dedicated to explaining about life in the Roman army, as well as about the armour and weapons that they used, with replicas of Roman artillery on display. There is also a 3D film set in a Roman tent and hosted by Roman centurion, Africanus, and a holographic teacher in a Roman classroom who explains more about on life on the edge of the Empire.

Directions & Accessibility: The Roman Army Museum is signposted from the main roads and has car parking on site. It is not possible to visit the actual fort site, which is to the south-west of the museum, although there are no significant features to be seen on the ground. The museum is fully accessible. A joint ticket can be purchased for the Roman Army Museum and Vindolanda fort.

Whitley Castle
Epiacum
Fort | Visitor Centre | Café | Toilets | Parking
www.epiacumheritage.org
NY 698 488 | CA9 3BG | systems.chestnuts.limes

Although the fort at Whitley Castle (better known as Epiacum) is not part of Hadrian's Wall or the Stanegate, it has some of the best-preserved defences of the forts in England. Only a half hour drive south of the Wall from Haltwhistle, it really is worth taking a slight detour to explore this fantastic undeveloped and rural site.

Epiacum sits on the Maiden Way, an old Roman road that connects the site to the fort at Carvoran (and now home to the Roman Army Museum). Surrounded by a series of defensive ditches and ramparts, with four of each surviving, and some indication of up to seven on the western side, the fort itself is unusual because it is rhomboid or diamond shaped. The site owes the excellent preservation of the defences because of its remoteness, although there are no traces of the internal buildings.

The area is known for lead mining in the post-Roman period, and although no evidence of Roman mining has yet been found here, archaeologists think this is the reason the fort was built at Whitley Castle. This idea is supported by evidence from lead seals found at the nearby fort of Brough-under-Stainmore, which were inscribed with 'the mines', so archaeologists assume Epiacum is the likeliest location for these.

The fort has only been excavated once, at the end of the 1950s, although there was some earlier work just outside the defences in 1810, when the bathhouse was uncovered. Many artefacts have been recovered from the site, both through accidental finds and from the excavations, including an altar showing Hercules (which is now in Bedford Museum), and another discovered in 1837 that depicts Apollo, the sun god, and is now in the care of the Great North Museum in Newcastle. Pottery recovered during the excavations in the 1950s indicate the site was occupied at the same time as Hadrian's Wall was in operation, although it is not clear when Epiacum was first occupied. Outside of the fort, on the north side, there is some evidence for a small settlement.

Thanks to Epiacum Heritage, who look after the site, a research framework and conservation plan has been put in place, and there is an ongoing programme of non-invasive research taking place. A few years ago the site was geophysically surveyed, revealing many new features including at least ten barrack blocks and a granary towards the centre of the fort.

Directions & Accessibility: Epiacum is around a thirty-minute drive south of Haltwhistle, and located on the A689, just north of the town of Alston. The Pennine Way passes close to the site. Parking is available next to the farm shop and café – both are worth visiting for the local produce and homemade cakes.

The fort can be reached through a gate at the southern end of the car park, although there is no formal track and the hill is a little steep, and may not be suitable for those with

Defensive ramparts and ditches, Epiacum.

limited mobility, particularly in wetter weather. Dogs are welcome, but need to be kept on a lead as the route passes through fields, which usually contains livestock

There are several trails around the fort and surrounding area that can be followed from the car park, where leaflets are available. There are two digital walks, downloadable from the fort website, which explore the archaeology of Epiacum and the surrounding area. As well as the fort, there is also the Wellhouse Bastle, a typical borderland fortified farmhouse, which has been partly restored and contains displays focussing on Epiacum and the surrounding area.

The nearby town of Alston, reputedly the highest market town in England, is worth visiting for a snapshot of life in the North Pennines. With a good selection of shops, restaurants and cafés, there are also small hotels and bed and breakfast venues in the area, making it a good base from which to explore the western sections of Hadrian's Wall and the Stanegate. Alston is home to England's highest railway, which runs for 5 miles from Alston to the village of Slaggyford in Northumberland. The South Tynedale Railway is a community run heritage line that passes close to Epiacum (although you cannot see the fort from the train). Disembark at Kirkhaugh station for the short walk to the fort.

Hadrian's Wall: West

The dramatic and craggy outcrops of the central section of Hadrian's Wall quickly gives way to rolling hills, which gradually become flatter as the Wall makes its way towards the lands of the Solway Plain. As the Wall follows the valley of the River Eden and becomes

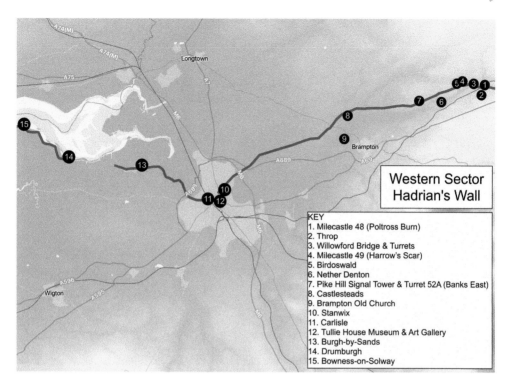

**Western Sector
Hadrian's Wall**

KEY
1. Milecastle 48 (Poltross Burn)
2. Throp
3. Willowford Bridge & Turrets
4. Milecastle 49 (Harrow's Scar)
5. Birdoswald
6. Nether Denton
7. Pike Hill Signal Tower & Turret 52A (Banks East)
8. Castlesteads
9. Brampton Old Church
10. Stanwix
11. Carlisle
12. Tullie House Museum & Art Gallery
13. Burgh-by-Sands
14. Drumburgh
15. Bowness-on-Solway

lost under modern Carlisle, it soon re-emerges as it heads towards the shores of the Solway Firth and Bowness-on-Solway where the Wall finishes, but the Roman defences continue.

* *

For the next set of sites, head into Greenhead village and take a right just past the café (signposted Gilsland), and onto the B6318.

* *

Milecastle 48 (Poltross Burn)
Milecastle | No Facilities | Parking
NY 634 661 | CA8 7BW | composer.obtain.bearable

Overlooking the picturesque Northumbrian village of Gilsland, Milecastle 48 is an important site in the history of studying Hadrian's Wall. Using the remains of Poltross Burn milecastle, scholars calculated the original height of Hadrian's Wall.

The well-preserved remains include the foundations of two rectangular buildings inside milecastle, which were probably barracks for soldiers, while in the north-west corner there are the remains of a small oven. The most interesting feature can be seen in the north-east corner, where the remains of three steps were used to project the course of the steps, which would have come to a height of about 3.66 metres. When adding in the height difference between the north and south sides of the milecastles, which was 4 metres, it suggests that the height of the building, and Hadrian's Wall, was 7 metres. However, this doesn't include any additional height gained from a walkway or additional battlements, which may have made the Wall even higher.

Poltross Burn milecastle.

Directions & Accessibility: Parking is available in a public car park at the western end of Gilsland village (signposted). From there, the milecastle (and the nearby Throp fortlet) are about a ten-minute walk away. The quickest way to get to the sites are to follow the Hadrian's Wall Path, which leaves from the north end of the car park (accessed from the main road). The path can be wet and boggy in places and involves crossing a small stream over a couple of planks of wood. Before the path passes across the railway line, there's a short stretch of the Wall at the northern end of the field, where the Narrow Wall, built on top of the Broad Wall, can be seen. Follow the path up to the railway line and turn left to the milecastle, or right (and across the style) to Throp fortlet, although there is little to be seen (see the next entry). Continue on the path, after the milecastle, until it takes you to a road in the village. Turning left here goes to the B6318, with the car park a ten-minute walk away, or take the alternative path, following the railway, passing a small section of the Wall, down some steps and across the stream, which is impressive when in full force, and then back up the steps. When climbing these up the other side, look out for the Wall ditch, which runs through the field on your left. At the top of the steps, head under the railway line back towards the car park.

Throp
Fortlet | No Facilities | Parking
NY 631 659 | CA8 2LX | outgoing.intention.circles

Located close to Milecastle 48 (Poltross Burn), Throp is a small, 0.3-hectare fortlet, which was built as part of the Stanegate fortifications. Excavated in 1910, the site has a typical layout for a fortlet, with a turf rampart surrounded by a ditch, and two entrances on the north-east and south-east sides. Several hearths, set against the ramparts, were discovered, but no internal buildings were discovered. This may have had more to do with excavation techniques of the time rather than an actual lack of structures. Pottery discovered at the site has indicated that Throp continued to be occupied in the early second century and through to the fourth century. Archaeologists have speculated that Throp was probably a supply or storage base, supplying the soldiers constructing the Wall and the units garrisoning the area.

Directions & Accessibility: Follow the directions for Milecastle 48, turning right and crossing the style after going over the railway line. The fort is up a steep hill and is unmarked, but is recorded on the Ordnance Survey map as a Roman fort. There are no significant remains, although the fort platform is partially visible.

Willowford Bridge & Turrets 48A (Willowford East) & 48B (Willowford West)

Wall | Bridge | Turrets | Milecastle | No Facilities | Parking
www.english-heritage.org.uk
NY 630 662 | CA8 7BW | groom.airliners.rang

Willowford is one section of the Wall that has a lot to offer visitors. Not only does the Wall stand impressively high, but there are the remains of two turrets in this section. Beyond this, visitors can follow the Wall down to the remains of the bridge, which carried the Wall over the River Irthing.

The Wall is immediately opposite the public car park in Gilsland, and can be followed all the way to the bridge. The Broad Wall foundations are clearly visible at the bottom of the curtain wall for most of the section, with the Narrow Wall sitting on top. There's also an opportunity to see some of the coarser stones that made up the core or centre of the Wall. On the other side of the Wall runs the ditch, which remains deep and now has the main access road for the farm running along the bottom. Shortly after Turret 48A, which is one of the best surviving towers, the Wall disappears briefly (due to agriculture and stone robbing), but soon reappears. At this point follow the path rather than the farm track. The second turret, which has not survived particularly well, is located by the farm buildings, towards the end of this stretch of the path. Turret 48B was excavated in 1923, with the excavators discovering charcoal and burnt timber, leading the excavators to speculate that the turret had an upper storey, which was set on fire and subsequently collapsed. Be sure to look out for the carved stone of centurion Gellius Philippus in the farmhouse's gable.

Continue on the path, following the Wall beyond the farm and make the long descent into the valley of the River Irthing. The remains of the bridge are at the end of the Wall. Since the Roman period, the river has moved course, and the remains are now about 70 metres from the current course of the river. Like some of the other bridges on Hadrian's Wall, this bridge was initially only wide enough to carry a footpath. Access was controlled by soldiers stationed in a tower next to the bridge. The bridge was excavated in the twentieth century, with archaeologists discovering that the bridge was damaged by flooding and subsequently repaired once at some unknown time, and then towards the end of the second or beginning of the third century. At this point the bridge was extended to the west and converted to take a road across the river.

Willowford East turret.

To visit Milecastle 49 (Harrow's Scar), visitors can follow the path south towards the river, where a modern bridge crosses the Irthing.

Directions & Accessibility: From the entrance to the car park in Gilsland, take a right towards the village and then take the track for Willowford Farm on the immediate left by the cottage. The track, which is part of the Hadrian's Wall Path, is signposted. It is a farm track and is stony in places, so may not be suitable for everyone with mobility issues. There are many steps down to the bridge site. Continuing on the path, and crossing the river over the new bridge, takes visitors to Milecastle 49 (Harrow's Scar), although there is a particularly steep walk up to the site (see the next entry).

Milecastle 49 (Harrow's Scar)
Wall | Milecastle | No Facilities | Nearby Parking
www.english-heritage.org.uk
NY 620 664 | CA8 2LX | clear.truck.stung

The remains of Milecastle 49 are notable because it is here that the Turf Wall originally began (or ended). Excavations in the 1950s confirmed that before the stone milecastle was built, its predecessor was constructed from turf. The stone milecastle was repaired in the third century, although it is not clear what caused the damage. There was some evidence of internal buildings, probably barracks for the soldiers patrolling and guarding this section of the Wall.

From here, the Wall continues to the fort at Birdoswald. While the Wall, which survives up to ten courses high at this point, is on the left, the space on the right was home to the large civilian settlement surrounding the fort, which stretched most of the way to the milecastle.

Directions & Accessibility: Harrow's Scar can either be reached by following the path from Willowford (see the previous entry) across the bridge and then make the incredibly steep climb up to the milecastle. Alternatively, it's possible to park at Birdoswald fort (pay and display) and turning left at the top of the hill from the car park, which takes visitors along one of the best sections of the Wall to the Harrow's Scar, around a ten-minute walk.

Birdoswald

Banna (horn or peak)
Fort | Museum | | Café | Toilets | Parking | Charge
www.english-heritage.org.uk
NY 615 662 | CA8 7DD | remarked.education.tile

Birdoswald is undoubtedly the best preserved of the forts along the western section of Hadrian's Wall. It is one of the longest occupied sites since the Roman period, with only a brief gap of a couple of hundred years when the site was probably unoccupied. With the longest surviving stretch of Hadrian's Wall to the west, and an equally impressive length to the east, Birdoswald is also the one fort to see if you're exploring north-west England.

Built on a promontory that falls away to the valley of the River Irthing on the north side of the site, Birdoswald has been excavated on several occasions throughout the nineteenth, twentieth and twenty-first centuries, as well as being subjected to extensive geophysical survey, and even an episode of *Time Team*, making it one of the best understood, but also one of the most complex Roman sites on Hadrian's Wall. A wide range of artefacts have been found at the fort, and the surrounding area include panels from a Roman tent. These were found in an enclosure, a little to the south of the fort, which may have been the site of a Roman camp occupied by builders of the Turf Wall. The original fort was constructed from turf with timber buildings and sat astride the Turf Wall. However, when they rebuilt the Wall in stone, they also rebuilt the fort, but had to move the latter further forward to accommodate the new footprint of the fortification. The *vallum* ran around the fort to the south, except this was filled in shortly after being dug. Initially, the fort had one defensive ditch, with a second dug in the latter half of the second century, but recent geophysical survey work has identified the traces of a third ditch at the south-west corner. However, most of the feature has eroded and the archaeology has been lost.

On the outside of the fort, just after the entrance to the courtyard, are the remain of the north-west corner and guard tower. At some point it was converted into a cookhouse and the remains of several circular ovens can be seen in the ruins. Within the ticketed part of the site, the remains are well signposted, but there are some highlights worth seeking. Immediately in front of the seventeenth-century farmhouse are the remains of a bastle house, a post-Roman fortified house that protected the inhabitants from Scottish Border reivers. Opposite the bastle house, on the other side of the path, are the late second-century granaries, with their distinctive buttresses on display. In two columns, running down the centre of the granary are a series of large wooden posts. These represent the timber supports for a large hall, which was discovered during excavation of the site. The hall was built in the ruins of the Roman fort sometime around or after the fifth century, long after the Romans had left Britain. The size of the postholes suggests that this was a substantial building, with archaeologists speculating that it was home to a local warlord, someone who had the power and money to build such a large hall.

As well as the excavated areas with visible remains, it is possible to explore the rest of the fort, although the ground can be uneven. As one of the best-preserved forts on the Wall, the outer walls of the fort are particularly impressive, standing up to seven and eight courses in places, with the remains of the southern gates being quite substantial. However, the gate to look at is on the east side, where one portal has been blocked up. The reasons for this are unclear, but perhaps it was to make the fort more secure against enemies, or possibly because there was not enough traffic going through the fort to warrant two entrances and soldiers to guard it. The fort has several smaller side gates, with wheel ruts visible at the western one showing that it was used by heavy carts. The site continued to be occupied after the Roman period, with construction of the timber building, and evidence from the west gate, which is by the hall, revealing evidence of activity in the early medieval period, and possibly as late as the fifteenth century. Many of the finds from the fort can be seen at Tullie House Museum in Carlisle.

English Heritage and Newcastle University are undertaking a series of archaeological investigations at the site over several years. The excavations are mainly focussing on the civilian settlement on the east and west sides of the fort, although other work is also being undertaken. Artefacts recovered from the site during this work can be seen in the onsite Education Centre, with tours of the excavations taking place daily while they are ongoing in the early summer months. There is more information on the Birdoswald website.

Directions & Accessibility: Birdoswald itself is signposted from the main routes and easy to find. Parking (pay and display) is available a little way to the east of the site, but involves

Birdoswald.

a steep climb up a footpath to the fort. Disabled parking is available closer to the fort, and the main part of the site is accessible via gravel paths. Visitors with limited mobility may find accessing the non-excavated parts of the fort more difficult.

Following the remains of Hadrian's Wall eastwards from Birdoswald will eventually, after about a kilometre, take visitors to Milecastle 49 (Harrow's Scar) and Willowford Bridge and another surviving section of Hadrian's Wall (see previous entry), but are aware of the very steep path down to the river valley.

* *

One of the longest stretches of visible remains of Hadrian's Wall runs from Birdoswald Roman fort westwards, with the minor road running alongside it for most of this length, although eventually the Wall becomes a more of a grassy mound running parallel with the road, with occasional glimpses of turret on the north side of the road, including 51B (Lea Hill), which was excavated in the 1950s. The section of Wall at Hare Hill may look impressive, but the facing stones were added in the nineteenth century. The vallum, which runs to the south of the road, can be seen around 20 metres to the south of the road as a series of grassy dips, and is not visually as impressive as other sections further east.

Several of the farms on the road run refreshment sheds, where you can buy drinks and sweets using an honesty system. These tend not to be open out of season, but a quick search online will reveal more details.

* *

Nether Denton
Fort | No Facilities | Limited Parking
NY 595 646 | CA8 2LX | enjoyable.dissolves.mountain

Nether Denton.

Overlooking a bend in the River Irthing, the fort at Nether Denton, by the village of Chapelburn, partly lies underneath the church of St Cuthbert and the adjoining rectory. There are no remains to be seen, although the artificial platform on which the fort was built is just visible from the main road. Aerial photography has shown the extent of the site and defences, with indications of a large settlement around the site. There are some signs that the settlement may have continued in use after the fort was abandoned.

Look out for the reused Roman altar, which is by the entrance to the church. Also located here is the grave of archaeologist F. G. Simpson, who died in 1955. Simpson was Director of Archaeological Field Research at Durham University and undertook a large amount of research into Hadrian's Wall and excavated several important sites.

Directions & Accessibility: Nether Denton is a rural site, but only a fifteen-minute drive from Gilsland (see Willowford entry). From the car park at Gilsland, head west and after several kilometres, you'll come to the hamlet of Chapelburn. Take the first right after the hamlet to the church. There is a small wooden sign at the junction pointing to the church. There is limited space for parking outside the churchyard.

Pike Hill Signal Tower & Turret 52A (Banks East)
Tower | Turret | No Facilities | Parking
NY 575 647 | CA8 2JH | hinders.locate.catapult

Although the remains of Pike Hill are not the most dramatic (they were destroyed during work on the road in the 1870s), they are quite important for understanding early Roman activity in the area. When excavated, a timber tower was found underneath the stone tower that can be seen today. The timber tower predates Hadrian's Wall and acted as a relay station to enable soldiers on the Stanegate to signal to nearby sites at Gillalees Beacon and Barrock Fell. When the Turf Wall was built, the tower was built into it, and then incorporated into the stone wall when its predecessor was replaced. The 1930s excavations showed the tower was still in use in the late fourth century.

Slightly further west of Pike Hill and the car park is another section of Hadrian's Wall, which has the remains of Turret 52A set in them. One of the earliest sections of the Wall to be preserved by the state in the 1930s, the turret remains one of the best examples on the Wall. From this section, it is also possible to see traces of the *vallum* running little way to the south.

Directions & Accessibility: Located close together, if you're coming from the east, Pike Hill will be the site you first encounter on the south side of the road. It is easier to continue on for about half a kilometre where there's a small car park. The path to the tower is accessed through a gap in the wall on the south-east side of the car park, and runs parallel with the road. The turret is a couple of metres on from the car park to the west.

**

After the remains of the turret at Banks East, the road continues for a little way before diverging from the line of Hadrian's Wall at the hamlet of Banks. A slight detour to the south will take you to Lanercost Priory (NY 555 637 | CA8 2HQ | riverbed.ahead. fatigued), another English Heritage that has a good café, and a good place to take a break from Roman archaeology and Hadrian's Wall, although a lot of the stone from the Wall and Birdoswald fort was used in the priory's construction. Look out for the three Roman altar stones in the undercroft. There are no significant remains to be seen between Turret 52A and Castlesteads Roman fort.

**

Castlesteads

Camboglanna (bank at the bend)
Fort | No Access
NY 512 634 | CA8 2AU | throat.revision.corporate

Castlesteads can be considered one of the least exciting Roman forts on Hadrian's Wall because in 1791, the site was largely cleared to become formal gardens for nearby Castlesteads House. Until that time, accounts indicate there were substantial remains of the fort to be seen. Now there are no visible remains other than a slight rise at one end of the fort platform.

There has been limited excavation of the site in the twentieth century, along with geophysical survey, with the latter discovering the *vallum* running to the south of the site, but like the rest of the site, this is not visible on the ground. To the south of the *vallum*, the geophysical survey detected a small civilian settlement. Finds from the site can be seen in Tullie House Museum, Carlisle.

Directions & Accessibility: The site is in private ownership and cannot be accessed.

Brampton Old Church

Fort | No Facilities | Parking
NY 509 614 | CA8 2AA | husbands.birdcage.likes

Set above the banks of the River Irthing, Brampton Old Church is the delightful setting for this Stanegate fort. Covered by an old cemetery, there are no Roman remains to be seen, while the small church, St Martin's, was constructed from stones from the fort, with some Roman stones still visible in the walls.

Limited archaeological work has been undertaken at the site, although it was excavated in the 1930s and 1960s, with pottery kilns found during the investigations. Nearby, a stash of blacksmithing tools was found, stuffed down a well along with pieces of cart and agricultural equipment, all of which can now be seen at Tullie House Museum in Carlisle. Like most of the forts on the Stanegate and on Hadrian's Wall, evidence for a civilian settlement has been found by the fort, with timber buildings recently discovered, although little more is known about this part of the site.

Directions & Accessibility: The fort is located underneath Brampton Old Church, which is to the west of the town. The site is at the end of Old Church Lane, which is next to Kirby Moor School. There is limited parking outside the church, and there are no visible remains and no paths beyond the church, although the ground is grassy and gentle in most parts of the site.

Brampton Old Church.

**

Westwards from Castlesteads fort, the line of the Wall and the vallum head towards the fort at Stanwix, underneath modern Carlisle, and there are few visible remains in the landscape. The vallum is visible in a few places, but the Wall, milecastles and turrets have been destroyed by agricultural works and stone robbing.

Few modern roads follow the Wall, and it is only really possible to see these sections and follow the line of the monument by walking the Hadrian's Wall Path from this point onwards. The course of the Wall runs to the north of Carlisle airport before meeting up with a minor road at Wall Head, then continues to Walby where the road joins the A69. At this point, the Hadrian's Wall Path diverges from the line of the Wall, and walkers can continue on the path rather than following the minor road, as the former heads south onto a short stretch of Stanegate before following the River Eden and into Carlisle and the location of Carlisle fort (on the Stanegate) and Stanwix fort (on Hadrian's Wall).

**

Stanwix
Uxelodunum/Petriana (high fort/Prefect of the ala Petriana)
Fort | No Facilities | On Street Parking
NY 401 570 | CA3 9DP | gift.among.librarian

Long since buried by the modern city of Carlisle, the Hadrian's Wall fort of Stanwix lies underneath the suburb, church and house of the same name. The only part of the fort which survives, and can be seen, is a small section of the north wall of the fort, which is in the grounds of the Cumbria Park Hotel.

The fort is the largest on Hadrian's Wall. Pockets of excavation have taken place throughout the twentieth century and more recently. These have enabled archaeologists to locate the gates of the fort, some of the internal buildings, the civilian settlement, several cemeteries and the course of Hadrian's Wall and the *vallum*. As most of the site is under urban development, it has not been possible to get an idea of when the site was first built, but the discovery of a small turf mound in the playground of a nearby primary school seems to suggest the earliest fort was a turf and timber build, which implies it was built around AD 122. That fort was replaced by a stone fort around the 160s. Exploratory work on the site in the 1930s led to the discovery of one of the stone fort towers, which was on top of the edge of the Wall ditch, indicating that Stanwix fort was added to the Wall after the latter had been built. This fort was remodelled on several occasions between the second and fourth centuries. Excavations north of Stanwix, and beyond Hadrian's Wall, has led to the discovery of a paved area, ditch and timber, dating to the second to fourth centuries, on the main road north to Scotland. Similar activity has been noted to the north of Hadrian's Wall at Benwell, by Newcastle. Archaeologists are unsure what the building was for, or why it was north of the Wall in seemingly hostile territory. Evidence for a civil settlement at Stanwix has been found to the west of the fort, while on the east side timber buildings have been found. So far there's been no evidence for occupation of the site between the post-Roman and medieval periods.

From 2017 onwards a series of excavations have been taking place at Carlisle Cricket Club (NY 397 566 | CA3 9NS | rental.fact.ranges) where a Roman bathhouse has been discovered during construction works. It was probably associated with the fort given its proximity to the site. The bathhouse may have been founded in the third century and remodelled in the following century. There has also been some evidence of activity in the building in the fifth century, but as excavations are ongoing, the story may change if new datable evidence comes to light. Some of the finds are on display in Tullie House Museum, and the excavations are due to continue for several years, with tours available in the summer months.

Directions & Accessibility: There are no visible remains to be seen.

Carlisle

Luguvalium (strong through Lugus)
Fort | No Facilities | Parking Nearby
www.english-heritage.org.uk
NY 396 562 | CA3 8UR | swim.bunk.swear

Occupying a position overlooking on the River Eden, and now partly underneath Carlisle Castle, the A595 and Tullie House Museum, the Roman fort at Carlisle was occupied by cavalry soldiers. Excavations mainly undertaken from the 1970s onwards have shown the shape and size of the fort, and found the barracks and several other internal buildings (under the grassy area in front of the castle).

Carlisle Castle.

The fort was under construction from AD 72, before the first major campaign in Scotland was launched under Agricola. Around AD 105, the fort was dismantled and the timbers burnt in a series of bonfires. The fortification was replaced by another timber fort, which itself was demolished around 140, and the site was abandoned until a new fort was built in stone in the third century. The last fort seems to have been occupied until the Romans officially departed Britain in the early fifth century.

To the south of the fort was an annexe or extension to the fort where industrial activity took place from the 70s until the early second century, when *mansio*, a sort of imperial hotel, was built in this space. There is evidence suggesting a large civil settlement surrounding the south, east and west sides of the fort, along with cemeteries in these areas. There is also some evidence, such as the discovery of V-shaped defensive ditches, which have been found during modern development, that have led some archaeologists to speculate that there were additional Roman forts in the area, which have subsequently been lost to urban development.

Directions & Accessibility: Although there are no remains to be seen, it is worth visiting Carlisle Castle (managed by English Heritage) and Tullie House Museum (see the next entry), both of which are built on top of the Roman fort and have a full range of facilities. There is a large car park (pay and display) on the east side of the castle. Due to the nature of the site, there is limited accessibility at the castle.

Tullie House Museum & Art Gallery
Museum | Café | Toilets | Parking Nearby | Charge
www.tulliehouse.co.uk
NY 397 560 | CA3 8TP | bigger.jaws.stable

Tullie House Museum, a hidden treasure in the heart of Carlisle, sits on top of Hadrian's Wall and the southern half of Carlisle fort. The museum occupies an old Jacobean mansion, and houses a large collection of archaeological objects relating to the Romans in the north-west of England. The museum has an extensive collection of Roman sculptures and inscriptions, including various impressive tombstones from the Wall and other nearby Roman sites. Finds from the original excavations of Carlisle fort in 1893, and the twentieth century, include a wide range of everyday domestic objects and weaponry used by Roman civilians and the military personnel based in the area. In the gardens, the line of Roman road is laid out, and there is a recreation of an indigenous shrine. There's even a life-size replica of the Turf Wall on display.

As well as objects from Roman Carlisle, the museum also has displays of objects from before and after the Romans, including many pieces from medieval Carlisle. A visit to Tullie House can take around three hours.

Directions & Accessibility: The museum is opposite Carlisle Castle, which itself sits on top of the Roman fort and is also worth a visit. The museum has a range of facilities, organises regular events for families and adults, and is fully accessible. The Roman collections are in the basement and on the first floor. The museum also has an excellent café.

The extensive second-hand bookshop, Bookcase (www.bookcasecarlisle.co.uk), has a vast selection of books on the archaeology of the city and Hadrian's Wall, as well as copies of the transactions of the local archaeology society. Just around the corner from Tullie House, it is worth visiting.

**

From Carlisle westwards, there are few visible remains of the Wall and vallum, although the line of both are known for most of the stretch between Carlisle and the end of the Wall at Bowness-on-Solway. Although few of the milecastles have been discovered, archaeologists have speculated as to their locations. A small stretch of vallum can be seen among the pylons to the rear of the Burgh Road Industrial Estate, and visible from the western end of Burgh Road, although it is not particularly remarkable.

**

Burgh by Sands
Aballava (apple or orchard)
Fort | No Facilities | On Street Parking
NY 328 591 | CA5 6AT | flip.statement.hung

Beyond Carlisle, to the west, we know less about the fortifications and the line of Hadrian's Wall than we do for its eastern and central counterparts, although this is changing as work is undertaken by archaeologists to fill in the gaps in our knowledge. The fort underneath the village dates to the Hadrianic period, although there are two others close by, but the exact dates of when these were founded and occupied is unclear, although Burgh I was probably operational before the Wall was built.

The modern road through the village follows the line of the original Roman road through the fort. Stone from the fort has been reused in many of the modern buildings, including the church. Archaeologists have also found traces of a circular enclosure lying underneath the south-east rampart of Burgh I fort. This has led them to speculate that there was an early Roman watch tower on the site predating Hadrian's Wall. Limited excavation has taken place at the fort, although a barrack block was discovered in the 1920s when a new burial ground was being created. To the east and west sides of the fort was a civilian settlement, although this could belong to Burgh II, one of the other nearby forts. The bathhouse for the fort was on the south side of the village, but this was destroyed in first half of the nineteenth century when a shipping canal was constructed to take goods from Carlisle city to the shores of the Solway Firth at Port Carlisle. The canal was later filled in and a railway line constructed along the remains. Although the railway line was closed decades ago, the line of this can still be seen running alongside the Solway Firth and is easily mistaken for the remains of Hadrian's Wall. The church of St Michael, on the western side of the village, is almost 1,000 years old, and is perhaps best known as the location where the body of Edward I lay in state shortly after his death crossing the Solway Firth to campaign against the Scots. The church reuses much of the stone from the Roman fort.

Directions & Accessibility: The fort lies at the eastern end of Burgh by Sands, although there are no surviving remains to be seen, except for some Roman stones that have been reused in the walls of St Michael's Church.

St Michael's Church, Burgh-by-Sands.

** **

The course that the Wall and vallum took between Burgh by Sands and Drumburgh remains, for those most part, unidentified. It had been assumed that the Wall had been lost to coastal erosion at Burgh Marshes, but geophysical work has suggested the Wall stopped at the edge of the marshes – the Romans probably decided the marshes were enough of a barrier to prevent enemy attacks.

At the Burgh end, the vallum has recently been located through geophysical survey and actually lies about 40 metres south of its positioning on Ordnance Survey maps, and is visible, although barely, in the fields by the road. The Wall reappears to the east of Drumburgh, with excavation showing that the Turf Wall was used as a foundation for the Stone Wall. This work has also shown that the Wall was poorly constructed in places. Around this point, it is easy to mistake the remains for the old Carlisle to Port Carlisle railway for sections of Wall.

** **

Drumburgh

Congabata (dish-like)
Fort | No Facilities | On Street Parking
NY 263 598 | CA7 5DP | insurance.pylon.torches

The pretty village of Drumburgh is home to the smallest fort on Hadrian's Wall, which was originally constructed from timber and turf. The first fort was connected to the Turf Wall, but when it was rebuilt in stone, it was built on a slightly different alignment for some unknown reason. Archaeologists exploring the site through excavation and geophysical

Drumburgh.

survey have found the fort granary. When it was excavated, coins from the fourth century were found, indicating use of the fort into the fifth century. Stones from the fort have been reused in some of the buildings that can be seen today, while on the beach several large stones have been found, which archaeologists think may have come from a Roman harbour.

Directions & Accessibility: There are no Roman remains to be seen, and no dedicated car park within the village, but there are some roadside spaces that can be used.

**

From Drumburgh, the modern road mainly follows the line of the Wall before it reaches Bowness. Some milecastles and turrets in this section have been discovered and excavated, although there are no significant remains to be seen. As the road heads north, passing the turning to Glasson (on the west side), it runs by Milecastle 77 (Raven Bank), which was excavated in the 1970s. During construction work for a canal from Port Carlisle to the city, the Wall was dug up and found to be constructed on top of wooden piles, a technique that the Romans used to build on wet and marshy ground. As the road runs next to the water, the Wall is on the south side.

Just past the entrance to Glendale Caravan Park are the remains of Milecastle 78 (Kirkland), with the vallum just visible in the adjacent field, although hedging makes it difficult to see the minor earthworks. At Port Carlisle, the Wall takes a hard left away from the coast, while the vallum runs south of the village. Continue on the road towards Bowness, with the road on the left.

**

Bowness-on-Solway
Maia (larger)
Fort | No Facilities | On Street Parking
NY 223 626 | CA7 5AF | roosters.ranks.thousands

Marking the western terminus or end of Hadrian's Wall, the fort at Bowness-on-Solway is quite different to its eastern counterpart at Wallsend, with no visible remains and being located in a rural, waterside location. Although the village sits on top of most of the fort, the site has been intermittently explored by archaeologists.

The fort is the second largest on the Wall and would have accommodated a thousand soldiers. Surrounded by two ditches, the earliest fort was constructed from turf and timber, but was replaced in stone around the same time as the Turf Wall was replaced. It is not known when the fort was abandoned, although a coin from the latter half of the fourth century has been found at the site. There is evidence for a civil settlement on the south of the fort, as well as some signs of activity to the north-east.

Like Wallsend fort, Hadrian's Wall doesn't seem to have finished at the fort, with antiquarians in sixteenth and seventeenth century accounts recording that a spur or end section of the Wall continued for around quarter of a mile to the west of Bowness. Some archaeologists have even speculated that the Wall may have continued for up to a mile to the west, beyond the fort, although there is no evidence of this today. The picturesque church of St Michael sits on the south-eastern side of the fort and reuses Roman stone in its construction.

Directions & Accessibility: There is a small car park at the western end of the village, from where it is easy to explore the village and the beach.

St Michael's Church, Bowness-on-Solway.

Cumbrian Coastal Defences

From the western end of Hadrian's Wall, a different set of defences were constructed, running down the coast of Cumbria. In the northern section of these coastal defences, the Romans built a series of forts, interspersed with milecastles, and towers between these – a replication of the arrangements along Hadrian's Wall, but without a partition or curtain wall. The forts continue as far south as Ravenglass, but the smaller fortifications stop just south of Maryport, and archaeologists debate whether this system of coastal defences continued any further.

Many of the mile fortlets are noted on Ordnance Survey maps of the area, but there are few remains to be seen on the ground, with the site at Swarthy Hill (MF 21) being one of the best to visit.

Kirkbride
Fort | No Facilities | Parking Nearby
NY 229 571 | CA7 5HR | successes.recliner.diverts

Kirkbride fort lies to the north of the village, partly under the hamlet of Angerton and partly under agricultural land. There are no visible remains or even earthworks to be seen here. The fort predates Hadrian's Wall, and some archaeologists think Kirkbride marks the western terminus of the Stanegate, rather than ending at Carlisle fort. There has been

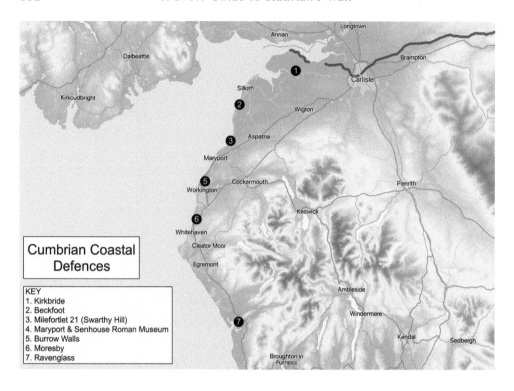

St Bride's Church, Kirkbride.

limited excavation at Kirkbride, with timber buildings revealed during one dig. Geophysical survey of the area has revealed a big civilian settlement, while aerial photographs of the site suggest that there may be an enclosure outside the fort, but this is not visible on the ground and archaeologists are unsure of what this could be.

Directions & Accessibility: There is limited on-street parking in Angerton, with the fort lying at the northern end of the hamlet. The fort is not signposted and there is no evidence of it on the ground.

Beckfoot
Bibra (brown or beaver river)
Fort | No Facilities | Parking
NY 089 488 | CA7 4LB | driving.detriment.jugs

There is nothing to be seen of the fort at Beckfoot, which is now underneath a field, but the site has extensive views of the Solway coast and across to Scotland. It was first excavated towards the end of the nineteenth century, with the outline of the defences of the traced, along with some of the internal buildings. An unrecorded excavation took place in the mid-1930s, and further work in 2011 when the bungalow on the north-west corner of the fort was being redeveloped. The site has been extensively geophysically surveyed, which has shown that there was an extensive civilian settlement surrounding the fort on three sides, with evidence of agricultural cultivation to the east, although this may not be Roman. There is evidence of a cemetery to the south-west of the fort, facing the beach, but unfortunately it is gradually being eroded.

Directions & Accessibility: A small car park is located on the west side of the B5300, a little to the south of Beckfoot farm and Rowanbank Caravan Park. The fort itself is about 25 metres south of the car park, on the opposite side of the road. The modern bungalow on the east side of the road sits just outside the north-eastern corner of the fort.

Milefortlet 21 (Swarthy Hill)
Milefortlet | No Facilities | Parking
NY 067 400 | CA15 6PB | propose.outnumber.pill

Located overlooking the Solway coast, Milefortlet 21 at Swarthy Hill was excavated in the early 1990s, giving archaeologists a good idea of what these sites originally looked like. It is also one of the better-preserved mile fortlets to visit, with the turf outline of the defensive bank and ditches still surviving as a low mound.

Discovered through aerial photography in 1968, the excavations of the 1990s discovered two entrances to the site on the east and west sides, while within the mile fortlet there were the remains of a square timber tower, which could have been around 10 metres high. There was also evidence for three small buildings on the south side of the interior, two with ovens and a hearth, while on the north side of the interior was a single building, probably a barrack, which had four doors that led to individual cubicles with a hearth in each one.

Directions & Accessibility: The fortlet is next to Crosscanonby Saltpans, an Elizabethan industrial site where salt was extracted by evaporating water mixed with sand from the

Swarthy Hill milefortlet.

adjacent beach. There are several small car parks on the coastal side of the road, although these are not signposted and are easy to miss. The fortlet is signposted and accessible by following a path through a field. It is about a ten- to fifteen-minute walk from either of the coastal car parks or there is a small layby by Crosscanonby Nature Reserve, which is on the minor road, signposted Crosby, which is the nearest to the site.

Maryport & Senhouse Roman Museum
Aluana (shining or brilliant)
Fort | Museum | Museum | Toilets | Parking | Charge
www.senhousemuseum.co.uk
Fort & Museum |NY 038 372 | CA15 6JD | swimmer.wonderful.soap

Maryport is the must-see site on the Cumbrian coast, with plenty to explore from one of the oldest museums in Britain, from its extensive collection of Roman altar stones to the remains of the fort, but also for the views over the Solway coast and south-west Scotland.

The first fortification on the site was probably a tower (23B), which makes up part of the coastal defences, although this seems to have been quickly replaced, around the time that Hadrian's Wall was being built, by the fort that can be seen today. Some archaeologists believe that there may have been an even earlier fort, along with a Roman harbour nearby, although no such sites have so far been found. Maryport is probably best known for the large number of altars that have been found around the site, with seventeen alone discovered in 1870 from a small area north-east of the fort. More recent work in the 2010s re-excavated these pits, finding both a new altar and concluding that these were the pits in which this and the previous altars were found. These were used as the foundations for massive timber buildings, which were possibly built by the Romans after the Hadrianic period. This later work also revealed a rectangular temple, with evidence suggesting that animals were sacrificed before it was built, sometime between AD 225 and 390, but probably earlier rather than later.

There was an extensive civilian settlement surrounding the fort, with the main concentration of activity being on the north side. Recent survey and excavation of this area shows that it was established in the Hadrianic period, around the same time as the fort, and continued to be occupied throughout the second century. A lack of pottery from the end of the third and the fourth centuries suggests either a reduction in the population as people moved away, or that the site was complexly abandoned. Interestingly, and unlike some other sites in the area, there was no evidence of post-Roman activity at Maryport.

The museum began life in the sixteenth century as a collection of inscribed stones gathered by local landowner John Senhouse, and which grew over the years as new discoveries were made, particularly when the stone from the fort was mined for the construction of Maryport town in the eighteenth century. By the 1960s the collection was almost forgotten about before attempts were made to save it. By 1990 it was once more secure and put on display in the present building, an old Royal Navy drill hall. Within the museum is a spectacular collection of Roman objects, ranging from carved altars to inscribed building stones. One to see is the curious and somewhat phallic, Serpent Stone, combining Celtic art with Roman symbolism as part of a funerary monument, and has a serpent on one side, with a human face on the reverse. The intention, by those who erected it, could have been to

Senhouse Roman Museum, Maryport.

protect the burials and cremations that surrounded it. The museum also has a replica of the *sacellum*, the room at the heart of a Roman fort that housed the standards and statues of the Emperor, and which was usually on top, or sometimes next to, the treasury, the sunken room, which can be seen at various Roman forts on the Wall. There is also a viewing tower overlooking the fort, which gives a great bird's-eye view of the site, along with the visible earthworks, as well as the surrounding area and across the Solway Firth to Scotland.

Directions & Accessibility: The museum has a small car park and is largely accessible to those with mobility issues, with more information on the website. Anyone planning to walk to the site from Maryport town should know the site is at the top of a steep hill. There is limited access to the fort itself, but it can be viewed from the museum, viewing platform, or the path that runs around the western side of the site.

Burrow Walls
Fort | No Facilities | Parking Nearby
NY 003 301 | CA14 1AU | demand.undulation.mats

Located almost halfway between the forts of Maryport and Moresby, the fort at Burrow Walls is one of the smaller coastal sites covering an area of about 1.2 hectares. Like several of the forts on the Cumbrian coast, Burrow Walls has been partially been destroyed by an old railway line cutting through the site. Although there are no significant features to be seen on the surface, excavations in the 1990s indicated that the foundations of the walls survive 2.5 metres below ground level. There were also two particularly wide (5 metres) ditches surrounding the fort. Pottery found at the site dated to the second century, and then

Reused Roman stone, Burrow Walls.

possibly again to the fourth, suggesting a pause in occupation of the fort. Although there are no Roman remains to be seen at the site, some of the stone from the fort were used to construct a medieval hall, the ruins of which are next to the fort, as well as a boundary wall on the east side of the field, which reuses Roman stone.

Directions & Accessibility: The ruins are visible from the path, a former railway line, which runs past the site and is accessible from Northside or Seaton, to the north of Workington. The fort is closer to the southern end and overlooks Siddick Ponds Nature Reserve (www. siddickponds.co.uk).

Moresby
Gabrosentum (goat path)
Fort | No Facilities | Parking
NX 982 209 | CA28 6PU | calm.blueberry.letters

The cemetery of the church of St Bridget sits almost on top of the fort at Moresby, while the church is just outside of the eastern fort gate. Other than the corners of the fort ramparts, which are visible in the field to the west of the cemetery, there are no remains to be seen here.

St Bridget's
Church, Moresby.

A building inscription from the site of the east gate has shown that the fort was built sometime between AD 128 and 138, although as Moresby is not located on a headland, unlike the forts at Beckfoot and Maryport, there has been speculation by archaeologists that it was not originally intended to be part of the Cumbrian coastal defences. There was a civilian settlement to the south of the fort, towards the modern village, while archaeological investigations have indicated that there is a cemetery to the south-east.

Directions & Accessibility: There is limited parking outside St Bridget's Church, although access may be limited access at certain times. Alternatively, there is on street parking nearby within the village of Parton – the fort is about a fifteen-minute walk to the north. The cemetery sits on top of the eastern section of the fort, with the rest of the site being fields, and is accessible through the gate in the wall at the western side of the cemetery.

Ravenglass
Glannoventa
Fort | Bathhouse | No Facilities | Parking Nearby
www.english-heritage.org.uk
SD 088 959 | CA18 1SR | drew.snuggled.armful

The village of Ravenglass is home to the southernmost Roman fortification on the Cumbrian coast, and although there is almost nothing of the fort to see, the bathhouse itself is impressive as it is the tallest standing Roman structure in northern Britain. The fort sits at the mouth of the River Esk and was likely to have been chosen because of the shelter that the river would have provided for shipping, although no evidence of a harbour has been discovered, possibly because the River Esk has eroded it and the sands have shifted since Roman times. Covering an area of around 1.4 hectares, the fort was surrounded by a single rampart and ditch, although there is slight evidence suggesting that there may have been a second ditch on the south side of the fort underneath the modern road.

There is limited evidence to suggest that there was an early Roman fortlet nearby, which was founded during the Hadrianic period. This has led some to suggest that the system of mile fortlets and towers extended beyond Maryport to Ravenglass, and possibly even beyond. However, this is all speculation and there is no evidence for the chain extending this far south. This has led archaeologists to question the purpose of the fort at Ravenglass, and it seems likely that supplies and troops were landed here for movement further east to the forts at Hardknott (Mediobogdum) and Ambleside (Galava). Another possibility is that the fort was a base for the intended invasion of Ireland, which was planned in the first century but never took place. The problem with this theory is that there is only evidence for activity at Ravenglass in the second century and again in the fourth.

In the nineteenth century, the site was divided by the construction of the railways from Carlisle to Barrow-in-Furness, simultaneously destroying a section of the fort, while protecting the rest of the site from the sea, which has and continues to erode the western section. The fort, along with the nearby bathhouse, have been investigated on a number of occasions, with the latter first explored in 1881. This was followed by excavation of the fort by Lord Muncaster in 1885, and then another set of extensive excavations in the mid-1970s. In the 1990s the fort was extensively surveyed, with further investigations more recently. This work has been enabled archaeologists to the interior buildings, as well as evidence for the civilian settlement on the north side of the fort. Excavations at

Ravenglass have revealed timber buildings inside the fort, although the remains of some of these showed that they were burnt down and reconstructed several times. It is difficult to know if this resulted from an accident or enemy attack, or merely because the fort was being remodelled, or even abandoned. The Romans regularly set fire to forts, as it was the quickest way to clear the site and stop them falling into enemy hands.

The bathhouse, known locally as Walls Castle, was a ruin by the early 1600s. An old story, told in these parts, says that the bathhouse was the original home of the Pennington family, owners of nearby Muncaster Castle. It seems an unlikely story, given that bathhouses do not have a layout that lends themselves to family accommodation, particularly given how small they can be. The bathhouse dates to the Hadrianic period and had a similar layout to others along the line of the Wall such as Chesters and Wallsend. The remains of the baths are impressive, and in some places almost stand to their original height. Some sections even have the remains of the original Roman mortar rendering still in place. It is amazing to think even these small sections have survived for 2,000 years!

Directions & Accessibility: The Roman sites are around a ten-minute walk south of the village and can be accessed by following Walls Drive. The first site you come across is the bathhouse on the left. Almost opposite the bathhouse site is a large, empty field, which is home to the fort. There are no visible remains, and the field itself only contains around two thirds of the site, with the railway cutting through the remaining part of the site, although that section, along with the rest of the fort, is not accessible. The fort site can be hazardous and overgrown, with many dips and depressions hidden by the undergrowth. Continuing down Walls Drive, and taking a right where the track forks, will take you underneath the railway and onto the beach. Caution is needed here as the sands can be soft with quicksand in places. Following the shoreline northwards, when the tide is out, takes visitors past the fort site and back towards the village. There are no facilities or parking at either site, although there is a car park (SD 085 965 | CA18 1SN | beaks.commended.legwork) and toilet in the village itself, along with several pubs and cafés.

As well as the Roman remains and walks along the beach, the other main attraction in the area is the Ravenglass and Eskdale Steam Railway, one of the oldest and longest narrow gauge railways in England. La'al Ratty (little railway), as it is known by Cumbrians, is over a century old and connects Ravenglass with Dalegarth for Boot, in the Lake District. It takes around forty minutes each way, and the line itself roughly follows the route of the old Roman road, which headed eastwards. The railway operates from March to October, although there are special trains running during autumn and in the run up to Christmas and New Year. It is a great experience and a chance to see the countryside around Ravenglass from a different perspective.

Another interesting visitor attraction worth a trip to is Muncaster Castle (www.muncaster. co.uk), which currently sits on an outcrop overlooking Ravenglass, and is reputed to be built on the site of a Roman tower. Home to the Pennington family from at least the 1200s, the present castle has its origins in the thirteenth century, although it has been significantly expanded, enlarged and remodelled several times since then. The castle also has extensive gardens that can be explored, with the oldest surviving feature being the Georgian Terrace, which was initially laid out in the 1780s, and are particularly renowned for the extensive collection of rhododendrons planted in the early twentieth century. Muncaster Castle is also renowned for its collection of ghosts and is reputedly one of the most haunted castles in England, regularly hosting spooky events.

Roman bathhouse, Ravenglass.

* *

Ravenglass marks the end of the known system of Cumbrian coastal defences, with no further forts or towers to the south. Some archaeologists believe there are more awaiting rediscovery or that some have been lost to the sea through coastal erosion. To the east of Ravenglass is a different story, with several Roman fortifications located in the heart of the Lake District. Heading almost east from Ravenglass, following the minor road through the village of Eskdale Green and going beyond Dalegarth, the terminus of the Ravenglass and Eskdale Steam Railway (see below), is the highest Roman fort in England at Hardknott (Mediobogdum). A narrow but passable road winds its way up the Hardknott Pass to the fort, on your left as you head east and before you reach the top of the pass. Dating to the Hadrianic period, the visible remains at this site include the fort itself, some of the internal buildings ,and the bathhouse, which itself is located next to the small car park. Heading out of the north-east gate of the fort, about a five-minute walk up the slope is a large cleared area, which is assumed to have been a parade ground for soldiers stationed here, with an artificial hillock on the northern side assumed to have been the platform where the commanding officer would stand barking out orders as the soldiers marched up and down. While the road trip up to the fort is not for the faint-hearted given the steepness, narrowness and sheer drops, especially if continuing beyond the fort, but it is worth it for the views, particularly those back towards Ravenglass. The site can be quite boggy, with steep drops on the north side of the site.

Continuing east on the road eventually takes you out at Ambleside, in the heart of the Lake District, the location of another Roman fort, Galava. The fort can be found off the A5075, sitting at the head of Lake Windermere. Owned by the National Trust, the fort is free to visit, although there is no parking at the site.

* *

Hardknott.

Outpost Forts

Not strictly part of Hadrian's Wall, these forts formed part of a series of outposts designed to secure the territories to the north of the Wall, and to intercept any troublemakers intent on invading the Empire. Some were founded and occupied at the same time as the Wall, but not all. Risingham was established almost 100 years later, under the Emperor Septimius Severus, which shows that the Wall was an important barrier and frontier for the Romans long after its original construction.

Risingham
Habitancum
Fort | No Facilities | On Street Parking
NY 890 862 | NE48 2RY | stack.complies.decompose

The well-preserved remains of the fort at Risingham are a must see for anyone exploring the landscape north of Hadrian's Wall. The fort, known to the Romans as Habitancum, was founded in the Antonine period, although there is a possible earlier fort underneath. The evidence indicates that it was destroyed or demolished around 197, before being rebuilt in the third century during the reign of the Emperor Septimius Severus, who campaigned in Scotland.

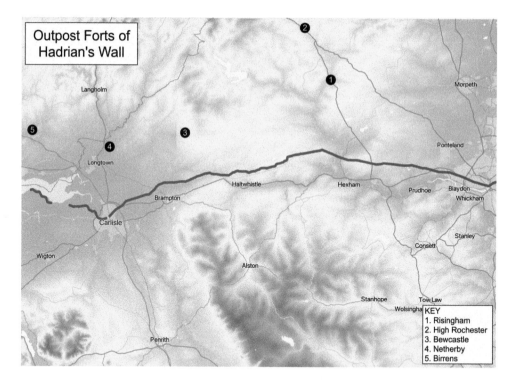

Limited excavation and survey work has taken place at the fort, but it was surrounded by four defensive ditches, although it has been difficult to see this because of post-Roman agricultural activity on the site. The only visible section of Roman stonework is a couple of courses of a corner tower on the north-eastern side of the site. Excavations in 1840 located the bathhouse, which was located within the walls of the fort rather than outside of it, which could suggest there was an indigenous threat to the building. The site was occupied long after the Romans had abandoned it, with traces of buildings and ditches still visible today. The dating of these buildings is unclear, but there is documentary evidence of a settlement at the fort as early as 1604, and possibly even earlier in the medieval period. The last resident of the fort site left their cottage in 1826.

As well as the fort, there is one final relic worth seeking: Robin of Risingham (see below for directions), the only known example of a Roman rock carving in this part of England. Located in an alcove, the carving is assumed to be of a native hunting god. The original carving was partly destroyed by the landowner several hundred years ago, although luckily antiquarians had recorded the carving before its destruction, with only the bottom half surviving, and showing a god holding a bow and hare. A replica, erected in 1983, is located near to the site of the original carving.

Directions & Accessibility: The fort is a short distance south-west of the village of Woodburn, and a path leaves from the village that passes the site (marked on Ordnance Survey maps), but the fort itself remains in private ownership and permission should be sought to access the site.

Robin of Risingham can be found around a mile and half south of West Woodburn on the south-east side of the A68, and is marked on Ordnance Survey maps of the area (NY

9014 8564 | *coverage.chair.developed*). *It is a short walk, over rough terrain, from the main road. There is no car park nearby, but there is space for one vehicle on the verge at the entrance to the path.*

High Rochester
Bremenium (place of the roaring stream)
Fort | No Facilities | On Street Parking
NY 832 986 | NE19 1RA | flopping.lizards.both

The fort at High Rochester was one of the more remote and exposed outposts for soldiers to be stationed to. Even today, it is difficult to imagine a more remote site and a bleaker place to visit, but despite its location in the heart of rural Northumberland, a lot is known about the site because of previous excavations, geophysical survey work and ongoing explorations of the site.

The earliest known activity from the site comes from geophysical survey, which showed an Iron Age settlement on the site, which was cleared in the first century, and a Roman turf fort was constructed on the site. As well as internal buildings of timber, there was also an annexe or secure enclosure built to the side of the fort, which appears to have been used for industrial activity. The site was then abandoned, and there is no evidence for occupation of the site when the Wall was being built, but in the second century, the Antonine period, a new, bigger fort is built on top of the old one, along with a new annexe, which has been excavated. A lack of finds from half of the annexe has led to speculation that it was used to park or store wagons. A building was discovered in the annexe, which may have been the original bathhouse, which was moved inside the fort walls in the third century, when the fortification was again reoccupied during the reign of Septimius Severus who also had parts of the Wall refurbished and campaigned in Scotland. Interestingly, an inscription found at the site records that the Bremenium Scouts were in residence, giving an indication of the purpose of having a fort in this area – to undertake reconnaissance and monitor the indigenous populations. The remains of a circular tomb are visible along the track to the south-east of the fort. Originally, this would have been beehive shaped, and was probably a tomb to some unknown but possibly high-ranking soldier.

Directions & Accessibility: The fort is a short walk north of the village of Rochester, where there is limited parking and is located close to the farm of High Rochester, which sits on top of the fort. The minor road to the farm cuts through the fort, from the south gate to the east gate, while a public bridleway heads to the north gate of the site.

Walking around the perimeter of the fort, there are various sections of the original fort walls that are visible, including part of a partially bricked up gateway on the western perimeter of the site. To the north-west of the fort, and also on a bridleway (which is best accessed from the track at the north end of the village, rather than from the fort itself), is a Roman camp that was probably a construction base for the fort site. The turf perimeter defences of the camp are visible on the ground. The Roman tomb is around a ten-minute walk to the south-east of the fort, crossing rough ground. All of the sites are marked on Ordnance Survey maps.

Bewcastle
Fanum Cocidii (shrine of Cocidius)
Fort | Museum | No Facilities | Limited Parking
NY 565 746 | CA6 6PS | mentioned.roofed.wins

Sitting partly underneath the ruins of the fourteenth-century castle and in the shadow of St Cuthbert's Cross, Bewcastle Roman fort is one of the more unusual sites in Britain. Rather than the usual playing-card shape, the defences at Bewcastle have been adapted to fit the natural terrain, and is almost hexagonal in shape. Partly excavated on several occasions throughout the twentieth century, the fort was founded during the reign of Hadrian, with occupation continuing in the Antonine period. In the early 2000s, the fort and surrounding area were extensively geophysically surveyed, helping to identify buildings that hadn't previously been excavated, although as the fort is not rectangular, it is much more difficult for archaeologists to guess which remains belong to which building. The surveying also noted there was no evidence for a settlement anywhere around the fort. This is unusual because almost all the forts associated with Hadrian's Wall have some sort of civilian activity nearby.

St Cuthbert's Church, Bewcastle.

Arriving at Bewcastle, it is difficult to miss the substantial surviving ramparts that surround the site, with the road to the church running through them, and still give the impression of how formidable a Roman fort would have appeared to the locals. The ruins of Bew Castle, which reuses stone from the fort, can be seen at the north-eastern end of the site, and although it remains in private hands, permission to visit it can be obtained from the adjacent farm. At the southern end of the site sits St Cuthbert's Church, with the adjoining graveyard home to the Bewcastle Cross and a small museum. The Anglo-Saxon cross is one of the finest surviving examples of this type of medieval relic, and is still in its original position, although the top of the cross has been lost. The ornate style, with its carvings, implies that the site at Bewcastle was an important religious centre in the post-Roman period. A small museum/visitor centre is located in a building next to the Bewcastle Cross and contains information on the site before the Romans, and how it developed once the fort was abandoned.

Directions & Accessibility: There is no dedicated parking at Bewcastle, but it is possible to park outside the entrance to the graveyard and explore the site from there. The museum is within the graveyard, in a small building to the west of the church, with the Bewcastle Cross between these.

Netherby
Castra Exploratorum (fort of the scouts)
Fort | No Facilities | No Parking
NY 395 715 | CA6 5PR | unfit.clothed.truly

The Roman fort at Netherby has been recorded by antiquarians in the sixteenth and eighteenth centuries, but modern examination of the site has been much more limited that most of the other sites associated with Hadrian's Wall. Until the most recent survey in 2017, most of what was known about the site was speculative, with modern archaeologists unable to find many of the features that had been recorded by antiquarians. This hasn't been helped by Netherby Hall, which sits on the Roman fort. When the hall was constructed, most of the visible remains of the fort and the earthworks were destroyed. There is some hope for the site, as some limited archaeological investigations have confirmed that some Roman remains still survive beneath the surface.

Directions & Accessibility: The fort sits within the grounds of Netherby Hall and access is limited, although the hall itself is now mainly holiday accommodation.

Birrens
Blatobulgium (flowery hill)
Fort | No Facilities | On Street Parking
NY 219 751 | DG11 3LG | cowering.dare.hails

Located a few miles over the Scottish border, the outpost fort at Birrens is another site that has an extensive history. There is some evidence for a first-century foundation date, although it was certainly in use during Hadrian's time as Emperor, and again under Antoninus Pius. It was also the first fort to be extensively excavated in Scotland, at the end of the nineteenth century. Subsequent excavations have taken place in the twentieth century, and more recently it has been geophysically surveyed.

The earliest fort on the site was a simple structure, a secure compound with a single bank and ditch defensive arrangement. A new fort was then built with a more complex arrangement of defences, up to five ramparts and ditches, which are still visible on the north side of the fort. There are a series of annexes to the south and west of the fort, and a possible *mansio* to the north-east, although that building remains unexcavated.

If visiting Birrens, it is also worth making the trip a few miles north to Burnswark. This large, flat-topped hill is visible for miles around, and can even be seen from Birdoswald Roman fort on Hadrian's Wall. Burnswark is believed to have been the site of a Roman siege, with two Roman camps on either side of the hill where the army may have bombarded the indigenous settlement on the summit with artillery as a substantial number of Roman lead slingshots have been found on the slopes.

Directions & Accessibility: There is no dedicated parking at the site, but it is possible to park close to the verge and not restrict traffic. Burnswark (NY 219 751 | lighters.worked.teach) is a twenty-minute drive north of Birrens, with off-road parking available in the forest next to the hill. The site is not signposted and access can be limited, and an Ordnance Survey map is recommended if you're going to explore the area. Visitors to Birrens and Burnswark are advised to make themselves familiar with the Scottish Outdoor Access Code, which permits roaming on most open land in Scotland (outdooraccess-scotland.scot).

Birrens.

6. Finding Out More

There are various ways to find out more about Roman archaeology, including Hadrian's Wall and sites in the North of England, including through local groups and societies, such as the Cumberland and Westmorland Antiquarian and Archaeological Society (www. cumbriapast.com), who publish their own *Transactions*, and the Society of Antiquaries of Newcastle upon Tyne (www.newcastle-antiquaries.org.uk), who publish *Archaeologia Aeliana*. Back issues of the journals for both societies can be found through the Archaeological Data Service (www.archaeologydataservice.ac.uk) or their own websites. Both societies organise regular lectures and events, many of which are available online. They also sponsor and support excavations and research into Roman activity and have a wealth of information. Archaeological work on Hadrian's Wall is regularly undertaken by teams from different research institutes, including the Universities of Durham and Newcastle, with the latter involved in ongoing excavations at Birdoswald Roman fort.

Societies and Groups

Arbeia Society
Council for British Archaeology
Cumberland & Westmorland Antiquarian & Archaeological Society
Roman Roads Association
Roman Society
Society of Antiquaries of Newcastle Upon Tyne

Websites

www.hadrianswallcountry.co.uk
www.perlineamvalli.org.uk
www.followinghadrian.com
www.www.english-heritage.org.uk/visit/places/hadrians-wall
heritagegateway.org.uk
www.northumberlandnationalpark.org.uk/places-to-visit/hadrians-wall/
www.visitnorthumberland.com/explore/destinations/historical-sites/hadrians-wall
Individual fort websites

Further Reading

Many books have been written about Hadrian's Wall, and there is not the space to detail them all here. The books listed here are a sample of some of the best volumes covering the Wall, many of which have been consulted in the writing of the *Short Guide*. Many antiquarian volumes covering Hadrian's Wall are no longer in print, but can be found online through www.archive.org.

Key Sources

Armstrong, D., *The Hadrian's Wall Military Way: A Frontier Road Explored* (Pewsey: The Armatura Press, 2021)

Bellhouse, R. L., *Roman Sites on the Cumberland Coast: A New Schedule of Coastal Sites*, Cumberland and Westmorland Antiquarian and Archaeological Society Research Series 3 (Kendal: Cumberland and Westmorland Antiquarian and Archaeological Society, 1989)

Bidwell, P. (ed.), *Hadrian's Wall 1989–1999: A Summary of Recent Excavations and Research* (Carlisle: Cumberland & Westmorland Antiquarian and Archaeological Society & the Society of Antiquaries of Newcastle Upon Tyne, 1999)

Bidwell, P., and Hodgson, N., *The Roman Army in Northern England* (Arbeia Society, 2009)

Bishop, M. C., *An Introduction to Hadrian's Wall: One Hundred Questions About the Roman Wall Answered*, Per Lineam Valli 1 (The Armatura Press, 2013)

Bishop, M., *An Archaeological Guide to Walking Hadrian's Wall from Wallsend to Bowness-on-Solway (East to West)* (3 Volumes) (Pewsey: Armatura, 2014)

Bowman, A. K., *Life and Letters on the Roman Frontier* (British Museum Press, 1994)

Breeze, D., *Hadrian's Wall*, English Heritage Guidebooks (London, English Heritage, 2011)

Breeze, D., *Hadrian's Wall: A History of Archaeological Thought* (Kendal: Cumberland & Westmorland Antiquarian & Archaeological Society, 2014)

Breeze, D. J., *J. Collingwood Bruce's Handbook to the Roman Wall* (Society of Antiquaries of Newcastle upon Tyne, 2006)

Breeze, D. J., *Frontiers of the Roman Empire: Hadrian's Wall* (Hexham: Hadrian's Wall Heritage, 2011)

Breeze, D. J., 'The Marking-Out of Hadrian's Wall', *Archaeologia Aeliana*. 4, 319–26 (2014)

Breeze, D., *The Pilgrimages of Hadrian's Wall 1849–2019: A History* (Kendal: Cumberland & Westmorland Antiquarian & Archaeological Society and the Society of Antiquaries of Newcastle Upon Tyne, 2020)

Breeze, D. J., and Dobson, B., *Hadrian's Wall* (London: Penguin, 2000)

Collins, R., and Symonds, M. (eds.), *Hadrian's Wall 2009–2019: A Summary of Excavation and Research Prepared for the Fourteenth Pilgrimage of Hadrian's Wall, 20–28 July 2019* (Kendal: Cumberland & Westmorland Antiquarian & Archaeological Society & the Society of Antiquaries of Newcastle Upon Tyne, 2019)

Hingley, R., *Hadrian's Wall: A Life* (Oxford University Press, 2012)

Hodgson, N., *Hadrian's Wall: Archaeology and History at the Limit of Rome's Empire* (Marlborough: Crowwood Press, 2017)

Hodgson, N. (ed.), *Hadrian's Wall 1999–2009: A Summary of Excavation and Research prepared for The Thirteenth Pilgrimage of Hadrian's Wall, 8–14 August 2009* (Kendal: Cumberland & Westmorland Antiquarian & Archaeological Society - Society of Antiquaries of Newcastle Upon Tyne, 2009)

Jones, G. D. B., and Woolliscroft, D., *Hadrian's Wall From the Air* (Tempus, 2001)

Potter, T. W., *Romans in North-West England* (Kendal: Cumberland & Westmorland Antiquarian & Archaeological Society, 1979)

Rivet, A. L. F., and Smith, C., *The Place-Names of Roman Britain* (Book Club Associates, 1981)

Tibbs, A., *Beyond the Empire: A Guide to Scotland's Roman Remains* (Marlborough: Robert Hale, 2019)

Symonds, M., *Hadrian's Wall: Creating Division* (London: Bloomsbury, 2021)

Welfare, H., and Swan, V., *Roman Camps in England: The Field Archaeology.* (London: HMSO, 1995)

Wilson, R. J. A., and Caruana, I. D. (eds.), *Romans on the Solway: Essays in Honour of Richard Bellhouse*, Extra Series XXXI (Kendal: Cumberland & Westmorland Antiquarian & Archaeological Society, 2004)

Wilkes, L., and Dodds, G., *Tyneside Classical: The Newcastle of Grainger, Dobson and Clayton* (John Murray, 1964)

Woolliscroft, D., 'Signalling and the Design of the Cumberland Coast System', *Transactions of the Cumberland & Westmorland Antiquarian & Archaeological Society*, 9455–64 (1994)

Maps

Contains OS data © Crown Copyright [and database right] [2020/2021] – OS Open Rivers, Open Roads, OS Terrain 50, and OS Terrain DTM 5.

Garland, N. (2020a): Hadrian's Wall – Frontier system. figshare. Dataset. https://doi.org/10.25405/data.ncl.11855592

Garland, N. (2020b): Hadrian's Wall – Forts. figshare. Dataset. https://doi.org/10.25405/data.ncl.11855532

Garland, Nicky (2020c): Hadrian's Wall – Roman Roads. figshare. Dataset. https://doi.org/10.25405/data.ncl.11806944

Garland, N. (2020d): Hadrian's Wall – The Cumbrian Coast. figshare. Dataset. https://doi.org/10.25405/data.ncl.11855580

Individual Site Sources

The list of sources detailed here contain an extensive, but not exhaustive, list of the main bibliographic records consulted in compiling the *Short Guide*. Other sources that have been consulted are included in the general reading list.

The sources are formatted as follows: Source Abbreviation – volume - (publication year) – pages.

Source Abbreviations

The following abbreviations are used for the sources consulted for the individual site entries. Full details of the publications can be found at the end of the *Short Guide*:

AA	*Archaeologia Aeliana* (published by the Society of Antiquaries of Newcastle upon Tyne)
BRIT	*Britannia* journal
BDHW	*Hadrian's Wall* (by David Breeze & Brian Dobson)
HWFA	*Hadrian's Wall from the Air* (by Barri Jones & David Woolliscroft)
HTRW	*Handbook to the Roman Wall* (by David Breeze)
HW89	*Hadrian's Wall 1989–1999* (by Paul Bidwell)
HW99	*Hadrian's Wall 1999–2009* (by Nick Hodgson)
HW09	*Hadrian's Wall 2009–2019* (by Rob Collins & Matt Symonds)
JBBA	*Journal of the British Archaeological Association*
JRA	*Journal of Roman Archaeology*
JRS	*Journal of the Society for the Promotion of Roman Studies*
RANE	*The Roman Army in Northern England* (by Paul Bidwell & Nick Hodgson)
ROTS	*Romans on the Solway* (by Roger Wilson & Ian Caruana)
TAJ	*The Archaeological Journal*
TCWAAS	*Transactions of the Cumberland & Westmorland Antiquarian and Archaeological Society*

Beckfoot: HTRW 385–397; HW09 201–204.
Benwell: AA 6 (1865) 153–155; 161, 169–171; AA 19 (1941) 1–43; AA 40 (2011) 131–153; HTRW 151–157; HW89 100–102; HW99 90–91; HW09 131–139.
Bewcastle: HTRW 97–98; HW89 196–202; HW99 170–171; TCWAAS 22 (1922) 169–185; TCWAAS 35 (1935) 1–29; TCWAAS 90 (1990) 139–146; TCWAAS 12 (2012) 81–92.
Austen, P. S., *Bewcastle and Old Penrith: A Roman Outpost Fort and a Frontier Vicus: Excavations, 1977–78* Cumberland and Westmorland Antiquarian and Archaeological Society Research Series 8 (Kendal: Cumberland and Westmorland Antiquarian and Archaeological Society, 1991)

Birdoswald: BRIT 30 (1999) 91–100; BRIT 35 (2004) 159–178; HTRW 294–307; HW89 145–161; HW99 127–131; HW09 186–190.

Wilmott, T., *Birdoswald Roman Fort*, English Heritage Guidebooks (London: English Heritage, 2018)

Birrens: AA 12 (1887) 101–111; HTRW 97; HW89 202; JRA 32 (2019) 459–477.

Macdonald, G., *Birrens and Birrenswark. Transactions of the Dumfriesshire and Galloway Natural History and Antiquarian Society* 11, 2nd, 55–67 (1894).

Robertson, A. S., *Birrens (Blatobulgium)*, (Glasgow: T. & A. Constable, 1975)

Tibbs, A., *Beyond the Empire: A Guide to Scotland's Roman Remains* (Marlborough, Robert Hale, 2019)

Bowness-on-Solway: HTRW 367–371; HW09 200; TCWAAS 88 (1988) 33–54.

Brampton Old Church: HTRW 455–456; HW89 162.

Burgh by Sands: HTRW 350–354; HW89 177–179; HW99 151–154; TCWAAS 94 (1994) 35–54.

Burrow Walls: HTRW 409–410; HW99 165; TCWAAS 55 (1955) 30–45.

Carlisle: BRIT 23 (1992) 45–109; HTRW 457–468; HW89 168–177; HW99 140–150; HW09 195–196.

McCarthy, M., *Roman Carlisle & The Lands of the Solway* (Tempus, 2002)

Summerson, H., *Carlisle Castle*, English Heritage Guidebooks (London, English Heritage, 2008)

Carrawburgh: AA 8 (1880) 20–39; AA 8 (1880) 88–107; AA 29 (1951) 1–92; AA 40 (1962) 59–81; AA 50 (1972) 81–144; HTRW 216–223.

Allason-Jones, L., and McKay, B., *Coventina's Well: A Shrine on Hadrian's Wall* (Chollerford, The Trustees of the Clayton Collection, Chesters Museum, 1985)

Snape, M. E., *Carrawburgh Roman Fort and Its Environs* (London, English Heritage, 1994)

Carvoran: AA 45 (2016) 17–36; HTRW281–283; HW99 124–127; HW09 182–184.

Castlesteads: HTRW 330–333, HW89 162, 164–165; HW99 136–139; TCWAAS 22 (1922) 198–233; TCWAAS 7 (2007) 15–30.

Chesters: AA 7 (1876) 171; AA 8 (1931) 219–305; AA 45 (2016) 37–117; HTRW 195–209; HW89114–119; HW99 108–110; HW09 152–155.

Bruce, Rev J. C., 'I. - On the Forum of the Roman Station at Cilurnum', *Archaeologia.* 46 (1) (1880), 1–8

Hodgson, N., *Chesters Roman Fort and the Clayton Museum*, English Heritage Guidebooks (London: English Heritage, 2016)

Chesters Bridge: AA 5 (1861) 142–143, 148; AA 6 (1865) 80; HTRW 191–194; HW89 119–120; HW99 107–108.

Corbridge: AA 6 (1865) 18, 161; AA 37 (1959) 1–31, 59–84; AA 45 (1967) 17–26; AA 5 (1977) 47–74; AA 37 (2008) 47–92; BRIT 31 (2000) 11–22; HTRW 191–209; HW89 111–113; HW99 97–105; HW09 146–152.

Bishop, M. C., and Dore, J. N., *Corbridge – Excavations of the Roman Fort and Town, 1947–80* (London: English Heritage, 1989)

Hodgson, N., *Roman Corbridge: Fort, Town and Museum*, English Heritage Guidebooks (London: English Heritage, 2015)

Denton Hall & Burn: AA 4 (1927) 109–112; AA 40 (1962) 135–143; AA 24 (1996) 1–56; HTRW 160–162; HW89 101–102.

Drumburgh: HTRW 359–361.

Great Chesters: AA 24 (1903) 19–64; AA 45 (2010) 37–117; HTRW 269–275; HW09 180–181.

Halton Chesters: AA 14 (1937) 151–171; AA 37 (1959) 177–190; AA 28 (2000) 37–46; HTRW 178–183; HW89 105–110; HW 99 95–97.

Dore, J. N., *Haltonchesters: Excavations Directed by JP Gillam at the Roman Fort, 1960–61* (Oxford, Oxbow Books, 2010)

Haltwhistle Burn: AA 5 (1909) 213; HTRW 446–449; HW09 178–180.

Heddon-on-the-Wall: AA 4 (1927) 109–121; AA 36 (1958) 55–60; AA 40 (1962) 135–143; HTRW 165–166; HW99 92–94; HW09 140–141.

Hexham: AA 5 (1861) 150–158; HW99 105–107; HW09 152.

Hodgson, N., *Roman Corbridge: Fort, Town and Museum*, English Heritage Guidebooks (London: English Heritage, 2015)

High Rochester: AA 1 (1857) 69–85; AA 13 (1936) 170–198; AA 33 (2004) 25–50; HTRW 100–102; HW89 188–195; HW99 168–170.

Bruce, Rev J. C., 'Account of the Excavations at the Roman Station of Bremenium 1855, *Archaeologia Aeliana*, 1 (1857)

Housesteads: AA 25 (1904) 193–300; AA 11 (1934) 103–120; AA 33 (2004) 51–60; HTRW 233–249; HW89 123–127; HW99 112–113; HW09 160–164.

Crow, J., *Housesteads: A Fort and Garrison on Hadrian's Wall* (Stroud: The History Press, 2017)

Crow, J., *Housesteads Roman Fort*, English Heritage Guidebooks (London: English Heritage, 2012)

Rushworth, A., *Housesteads Roman Fort – the Grandest Station: Excavation and Survey at Housesteads, 1954–95, by Charles Daniels, John Gillam, James Crow and Others* (English Heritage, 2009)

Kirkbride: HTRW 468–469; HWFA 66–67; HW99 160; TCWAAS 63 (1963) 126–139; TCWAAS 75 (1975) 58–90; TCWAAS 82 (1982) 35–50.

Limestone Corner: HTRW 232–215.

Maryport: HTRW 397–407; HW89 184–186; HW99 162–163; HW09 205–212; TCWAAS 36 (1936) 85–89; TCWAAS 77 (1977) 7–16; TCWAAS 87 (1987) 61–66; www.senhousemuseum.co.uk.

Breeze, D. J., *Maryport: A Roman Fort and its Community* (Oxford, Archaeopress, 2018)

Wilson, R. J. A. (ed.), *Roman Maryport and its Setting: Essays in Memory of Michael G. Jarrett*, Extra Series XXVIII (Kendal: Cumberland & Westmorland Antiquarian & Archaeological Society, 1997)

Milecastle 35 (Sewingshields Crags): AA 12 (1984) 33–147; AA 25 (1997) 61–69; HTRW 230–231.

Milecastle 39 (Castle Nick): See Sycamore Gap.

Milecastle 42 (Cawfields Crags): AA 4 (1855) 54; AA 46 (1968) 69–74; HTRW 263–266.

Milecastle 48 (Poltross Burn): HTRW 285–288; TCWAAS 11 (1911) 390–461.

Milecastle 49 (Harrow's Scar): See Willowford.

Milecastle 77 (Raven Bank): See Milecastle 78 (Kirkland).

Milecastle 78 (Kirkland): HTRW 362–364.

Milefortlet 21 (Swarthy Hill): HTRW 394–396; HW89 184; TCWAAS 98 (1998) 61–106.

Moresby: HTRW 410–413; HW99 165; TCWAAS 48 (1948) 42–72; TCWAAS 55 (1955) 30–45.

Nether Denton: BRIT 35 (2004) 159–178; HTRW 452–453.

Netherby: HTRW 9–100; HW89 202; TCWAAS 53 (1953) 6–39.

Newcastle Upon Tyne: AA 4 (1855) 82; HTRW 144–148; HW89 97–99; HW09 128–131; HW99 83–84; TAJ 178 (2021) 107–145.

Bailey, R. N. (ed.), *The Roman Fort at Newcastle upon Tyne*, 5 (Newcastle upon Tyne: Society of Antiquaries of Newcastle upon Tyne, 2002)

Peel Gap Tower: See Steel Rigg.

Pike Hill Signal Tower: HTRW 320–323; TCWAAS 29 (1929) 303–315.

Ravenglass: RANE 118–121; ROTS 95–101; TCWAAS 6 (1881) 23–26; TCWAAS 28 (1928) 353–366; TCWAAS 49 (1949) 15–31; TCWAAS 60 (1960) 1–12; www.ravenglassromans.blogspot.com

Potter, T. W., *Romans in North-West England* (Kendal: Cumberland & Westmorland Antiquarian & Archaeological Society, 1979)

Risingham: AA 13 (1936) 170–198; AA 43 (2014) 47–71; HTRW 100; HW89 187–188; HW09 214.

Rudchester: AA 1 (1855) 93–120; AA 32 (1954) 176–219; AA 19 (1991) 25–31; HTRW 168–171; HW89 103–104.

South Shields (Arbeia): AA 11 (1886) 83–102; AA 30 (2002) 173; AA 46 (2017) 181–220; BRIT 17 (1986) 332–333; BRIT 35 (2004) 121–157; HTRW 114–129; HW89 73–82; HW99 61–73; HW09 109–115; JBAA 25 (2018) 373–383.

Stanwix: HTRW 341–345; HW89 162–163, 166–168; HW09 192–195; TCWAAS 85 (1985) 53–70.

Steel Rigg: HTRW 258–261.

Sycamore Gap: HTRW 257–258.

Throp: HTRW 450–451; HW09 27–28.

Turret 26B (Brunton): AA 31 (1953) 165–174; HTRW 189–191; HW89 113–114.

Turret 29A (Black Carts): HTRW 211–212; HW89 120–122.

Turret 33B (Coesike): AA 50 (1972) 145–178; HTRW 226.

Turret 45A (Walltown): See Carvoran.

Turret 48A (Willowford East): See Willowford.

Turret 48B (Willowford West): See Willowford.

Turret 52A (Banks East): See Pike Hill Signal Tower

Vindolanda (Chesterholm): AA 8 (1931) 182–212; AA 41 (2012) 207–215; BRIT 47 (2016) 243–252; HTRW 430–445; HW89 130–136; HW89 130–136; HW99 113–123; HW09 164–177.

Bidwell, P., *The Roman Fort of Vindolanda* (London, English Heritage, 1985)

Birley, R., *The Making of Modern Vindolanda with the Life and Work of Anthony Hedley, 1777–1835* (Roman Army Museum Publications, 1995)

Birley, R., *Vindolanda: A Roman Frontier Post on Hadrian's Wall* (Thames & Hudson, 1977)

Wallsend (Segedunum): AA 13 (1985) 213–214; HTRW 114, 131–138; HW89 83–94; HW99 73–76; HW09 115–122.

Hodgson, N., *The Roman Fort at Wallsend (Segedunum): Excavations in 1997–8*, Tyne and Wear Museums Archaeological Monograph 2 (Newcastle upon Tyne (Tyne and Wear Museums, 2003)

Rushworth, A., and Croom, A., *Segedunum: Excavations by Charles Daniels in the Roman Fort at Wallsend (1975–1984)* (Oxford: Oxbow Books, 2016)

Walltown Crags: See Carvoran.

Whitley Castle (Epiacum): AA 37 (1957) 191–202; RANE 128–130; BRIT 44 (2013) 93–143; epiacumheritage.org.

Willowford: HTRW 288–293; HW89 141–145; TCWAAS 26 (1926) 429–506; TCWAAS 97 (1997) 57–62.

Index of Places